CLINICAL EFFECTIVENESS
IN PSYCHOTHERAPY
AND MENTAL HEALTH

ucation Centre Library

CLINICAL EFFECTIVENESS IN PSYCHOTHERAPY AND MENTAL HEALTH
STRATEGIES AND RESOURCES FOR EFFECTIVE CLINICAL GOVERNANCE

Editors

Susan McPherson
Phil Richardson
Penny Leroux

KARNAC
LONDON   NEW YORK

First published in 2003 by
H. Karnac (Books) Ltd.
6 Pembroke Buildings, London NW10 6RE

A subsidiary of Other Press LLC, New York

British Library Cataloguing in Publication Data

A C.I.P. for this book is available from the British Library

ISBN 1 85575 902 0

Edited, designed, and produced by The Studio Publishing Services Ltd,
Exeter EX4 8JN

Printed in Great Britain

10 9 8 7 6 5 4 3 2 1

www.karnacbooks.com

CONTENTS

CHAPTER FIFTEEN
Involving health service users

PART V: APPENDIX

ACKNOWLEDGEMENTS

Chapter Five (pp. 27–42), Richardson, P. H. and Hobson, R. P. (2000), "In defence of NHS psychotherapy". Article reproduced with permission from *Psychoanalytic Psychotherapy*, 14: 63–74. Published by Taylor & Francis Ltd, http://www.tandf.co.uk/journals

Chapter Seven (pp. 49–70), Richardson, P. H. (2000), "Evidence-based practice and the psychodynamic psychotherapies". First published in *Evidence in Psychological Therapies: a Critical Guide for Practitioners* by C. Mace, S. Moorey and B. Roberts (2000) London: Routledge, pages 157-173. Reproduced with permission.

Chapter Nine (pp. 85–88), Charny, M. (1998), "Audit and research—untangling the ball of string". Article reproduced with permission from *Interchanges*, November 1998, No. 1. (*Interchanges* was the *Journal of the National Centre for Clinical Audit* which has since been absorbed into the National Institute for Clinical Excellence.)

Chapter Ten (pp. 89–96), Charny, M. (1998), "Audit by any other name". Article reproduced with permission from *Interchanges*, November 1998, No. 1. (*Interchanges* was the *Journal of the National Centre for Clinical Audit* which has since been absorbed into the National Institute for Clinical Excellence.)

The table (pp. 74–75) by Firth-Cozens. Adapted from Jenny Firth-Cozens (1993) *Audit in Mental Health Services*, table 3.1 p. 26 published by Taylor & Francis Books, Psychology Press.

The table (pp. 116–118): First published in *Identifying randomised controlled trials of cognitive therapy for depression: Comparing the efficiency of Embase, Medline, and PsycINFO bibliographic databases (Appendix)*, by Watson R. & Richardson P. (1999). First published in the *British Journal of Medical Psychology* 72. Reproduced with the kind permission of the British Psychological Society.

The Achenbach forms CBCL (pp. 134–135) and YSR (pp. 136–137) © T. M. Achenbach. Reproduced with permission.

FOREWORD

Susan McPherson, Phil Richardson and Penny Leroux

"C linical Effectiveness", "Clinical Governance", "Clinical Audit", "Clinical Guidelines"—these terms are all vitally important to the UK government's quality agenda for the National Health Service (NHS); all are apparently about clinical practice and yet all lead to a fair amount of confusion for the average practitioner. There are numerous publications from the NHS, the Royal Colleges and various institutions which attempt to give guidance in these areas. While several of these relate to the field of mental health, few if any refer specifically to psychological treatment services. This book was originally developed as a resource pack and practical guide for clinicians at the Tavistock and Portman Clinics in London. The broad focus of the book is clinical effectiveness.

There is an overview of clinical effectiveness and related issues in Part I, which sets out the historical context, the definition and the various components. Essentially, clinical effectiveness is set out as a quality improvement mechanism with numerous components. It goes on to explore how psychological treatment services will best fit into this framework and apply the mechanism to its practices. Clinical audit is given a particular emphasis as it was perhaps the first component to be widely implemented across the country and hence has the most developed methodologies. The section includes two articles reproduced with permission from the original publishers and one new article written for this book by Arlene Vetere. These three articles cover discussions on issues relating to clinical effectiveness in psychological treatment services and are intended to raise discussion and emphasize that methodologies in the area of quality are not hard and fast, but constantly require careful consideration and appraisal.

Parts II–IV provide practical guidance on building a clinically effective service, focusing on three important contributions to clinically effective practice, which are clinical audit, outcome monitoring, and evidence based practice. It addresses subjects such as how to carry out clinical audit, how to introduce outcome monitoring and how to achieve evidence-based practice, including the use of clinical guidelines. Part V provides a source of materials referred to within the pack, e.g. examples of outcome measures.

It is hoped that this book will be useful to clinicians of all disciplines, involved in providing psychological treatment services, by providing methodologies for reflecting on practice and improving quality. It is not intended as a comprehensive guide to clinical effectiveness as some areas have been covered in more depth than others. We should underline that the generic principles described in the various guidance sections are applicable across the board in mental health services.

We would like to thank Ann Phoenix and Chris Evans for their detailed comments on an earlier draft, as well as the numerous other colleagues and referees who have offered individual ideas and suggestions about how best to present the material contained within it. We would also like to thank Arlene Vetere for her contribution to the book and the publishers who kindly gave permission for previously published articles to be reproduced here.

ABOUT THE EDITORS

Susan McPherson BSc (Hons) MSc was the Clinical Effectiveness Officer at the Tavistock and Portman NHS Trust in London between 1998 and 2000. She currently works within the Psychotherapy Evaluation Research Unit as a Research Psychologist.

Phil Richardson PhD CClinPsychol is Head of Psychology and Director of the Psychotherapy Evaluation Research Unit at the Tavistock and Portman NHS Trust in London where he also acts as the Trust Lead for Clinical Effectiveness and Evidence-based Practice. He is also Professor of Clinical Psychology at the University of Essex.

Penny Leroux (BSc) was the Clinical Governance Support Officer at the Tavistock and Portman NHS Trust in London between 2001 and 2002 and is now studying for a doctorate in clinical psychology at Salomons (Canterbury Christ Church University College).

PART I:
EVOLUTION OF A QUALITY AGENDA IN MENTAL HEALTH

CHAPTER ONE

The early years

Adopting tools: clinical audit

The quality agenda for health care in the UK is often thought of as starting in 1989 with the Thatcher government's white paper "Working for Patients" (DOH, 1989). However, this development of a government agenda is fairly recent compared to the enterprises developing from within the health care professions as early as the 1970s and from even earlier examples from the 19th century. The concept of "audit" was the first quality improvement tool to be adapted for monitoring and improving quality within health care. A Medline search for articles with the words "medical" and "audit" in the abstract or title finds 72 items published between 1970 and 1975. Many of these are American, but several are also British with 17 coming from the British Medical Journal or the Lancet (see *Figure 1*). This demonstrates that the idea was being explored and experimented with within the medical profession long before "Working for Patients" made the activity compulsory for medical professionals in 1989.

However, the concept of audit in health care is evident from as long ago as the Crimean War in the 1850s. Crombie *et al.* (1993)

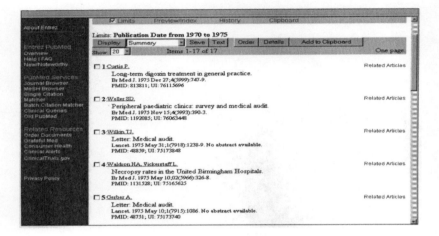

Figure 1. Medline findings.

describe how mortality rates at a British hospital near Constantinople became a political scandal, with an enquiry leading to a vote of censure on the government, after which the government fell. The Secretary of War subsequently ordered a detailed report on the conditions and quality of care at the hospital. These reports were compiled by Florence Nightingale who proceeded to lobby the Secretary of War and the Prime Minister, as well as generals and administrators, concerning the need for change. The death rate at the hospitals subsequently fell from 40 to 2%. Nightingale faced significant resistance to change, in spite of such appalling conditions. This may seem surprising, but nevertheless such resistance is not uncommon in clinical audit even today.

Moving into the 20th century, a high profile audit again came about through political scandal, this time relating to the high rate of maternal deaths. In 1929, the then Prime Minister, Chamberlain, set up a Departmental Committee to investigate maternal deaths. Eventually, this led to the establishment of the first national "Confidential Enquiry" in 1952, whose purpose was to collect data on all instances of maternal deaths from participating hospitals. Participation was not compulsory, but compliance was very high, possibly owing to the emphasis on confidentiality with no threat of disciplinary action. The Enquiry led to increasingly precise guidelines for patient management and at the same time much lower maternal mortality rates. These factors may have been causally related. One could also argue, however, that this increased regulation has led to greater "medicalization" of childbirth, with less individual choice for women and increased rates of surgical intervention. For example, caesarean sections in the UK have increased from 1% in 1949 to 16% in 1999 in spite of the World Health Organization guidance indicating that the rate need not be above 10% (Savage, 1999). This is an example of where meeting the immediate priority (i.e. reducing mortality) is only one important step towards increasing the overall quality of patient care.

Between 1975 and 1989 the Royal Colleges took a lead in formalizing the audit programme, setting up Working Parties to look at the use of treatments and standards of care. They produced policy statements and reports on the quality of care. For example, the Royal College of Physicians founded the Medical Services Group in 1977; the Royal College of Nursing established a working party on standards of care in 1978; the Royal College of General Practitioners issued a policy statement "Quality in General Practice" in 1985.

"Clinical audit"

Medical audit has, over the course of time, been re-termed "clinical audit" to reflect its relevance to all health professions instead of just the medical profession. Updating the Medline query described above to "clinical" and "audit" for the years 1995 to 2000 finds 1015 items (39 of which relate to mental health). The area of quality improvement has also developed beyond clinical audit to encompass a range of activities including "clinical effectiveness" and "evidence based practice".

Identifying ideals:
clinical effectiveness and evidence based practice

Clinical effectiveness

The national agenda for clinical effectiveness (CE) is also very recent, but, as with clinical audit, there have been several individual enterprises from as early as the 1970s. The most notable of these is

Archie Cochrane's paper written for the Nuffield Provincial Hospitals Trust on effectiveness and efficiency (Cochrane, 1972) in which he showed there were many different health care practices, but very little evidence to demonstrate whether these practices are effective or not.

> I remember at that time reading one of those propaganda pamphlets, considered suitable for POW medical officers about "clinical freedom and democracy". I found it impossible to understand. I had considerable freedom of clinical choice of therapy: my trouble was that I did not know which to use and when. I would gladly have sacrificed my freedom for a little knowledge. I had never heard then of "randomized controlled trials", but I knew there was no real evidence that anything we had to offer had any effect on tuberculosis, and I was afraid that I shortened the lives of some of my friends by unnecessary intervention. [Cochrane, 1972]

One reason why people were beginning to address these issues was the poor uptake of interventions that research had shown to be effective. A number of good clinical trials had been carried out, but it was only very slowly that the resulting evidence found its way into practice. A frequently cited example of this time lag is that of thrombolysis, which took 10–15 years to find its way into the textbooks, despite there being very good evidence from a number of clinical trials and meta-analyses that it was effective for myocardial infarction. Research also indicated that 10–20 years out of medical training, doctors were not practising according to best practice. There was evidence not only of a drop in knowledge over time, but also of unjustifiable variations in practice across the country.

Evidence based practice

Clinical effectiveness refers to a programme of quality improvements focused on populations and includes considerations of cost-effectiveness. Evidence based practice (EBP) is a close relative of CE. But it is more individually and clinically based. It refers to a way of improving the clinical quality of one's individual practice using a number of different methods and sources of evidence (e.g. efficacy, clinical effectiveness, and cost-effectiveness data).

Evidence based medicine traces its roots back to mid-century

Paris, according to Sackett, who defines it as "a conscientious, explicit and judicious use of the current best evidence in making decisions about the care of patients" (Sackett, 1997). The focus is on integrating the existing proficiency and expertise of the individual clinician with the most current clinical evidence. Emphasis on "current best evidence" implies that we have to start thinking about what we consider evidence to be.

Traditional means of obtaining information for use in clinical decision-making include training, textbooks, journals, continuing professional development, conferences, talking to colleagues, clinical acumen, reasoning from basic science, commercial materials, and also the media. Although, together, these provide vast amounts of information, there is likely to be extensive variation in the quality, type, and amount of information accessed and put into practice by individual clinicians. Without a more systematic way of informing clinicians about new evidence, it is unlikely that research will inform practice. There is, therefore, a danger of practice being exclusively opinion-based rather than evidence-based. Whilst there may be problems with attempting to work in an exclusively evidence-based way, to the extent that practice risks becoming tyrannized by external evidence, there are greater potential problems associated with opinion-based practice alone.

EBP is therefore about eliminating out of date and unnecessary variations in practice and treatment outcomes. It requires that clinicians be provided with a systematic way of keeping up to date with the relevant research literature, of being critically aware of research developments in order for them to make better informed clinical decisions. EBP requires that evidence or information about research gets to decision-makers, including commissioners of services, as well as individual clinicians who make decisions moment by moment for their individual patients.

References

Cochrane, A. (1972). *Effectiveness and Efficiency. Random Reflections on Health Services*. London: Nuffield Provincial Hospitals Trust.

Crombie, I., Davies, H., Abraham, S., & Florey, C. (1993). *The Audit Handbook*. Chichester: John Wiley & Sons.

Department of Health (1989). Working for Patients. NHS Executive.

Sacket, D. (1997). Evidence-based medicine. *Seminars in Perinatology,* 21(1): 3–5.

Savage, W. (1999). Caesarean section on the rise. *National Medical Journal of India,* 12(4): 146–149.

CHAPTER TWO

Political milestones

"Working for Patients", 1989

T here was no NHS agenda in this particular direction until the general election of 1987 when the Conservatives were coming up for their third consecutive term. There was much concern about hospital waiting lists, concern which continued more strongly after the election and led to the white paper "Working for Patients" (DOH, 1989) and the introduction of the internal market. "Working for Patients" saw the start of a major NHS initiative. It stated that all doctors should become involved in audit. A subsequent NHS circular in 1990 extended the coverage to nursing, and other health care professions have followed. Clinical audit has now become orthodox and many of the Royal Colleges stipulate that training posts for junior staff will only be recognized if there is an active audit programme within the unit. Although many health care professionals may regard these as dramatic developments, they are no more than the natural progression of a movement which had been gathering momentum over the previous 20 years.

When the Medical Audit programme began in 1989 with "Working for Patients", there was no mention of Clinical Effectiveness (CE)—

at that time it wasn't specifically on the Government's agenda. More significant was the beginning of the Research and Development Agenda with Research for Health in 1991 and then the formation of the Clinical Outcomes Group in 1992 (which has now been disbanded), headed by the Chief Medical Officer and Chief Nursing Officer. This led to the first executive letter about CE in December 1993. In July 1994 the Planning and Priorities Guidance for the NHS referred to CE for the first time. It stipulated that Health Authorities should be investing in programmes and interventions that are clinically effective and disinvesting in programmes of care that are clinically ineffective. This indicates that, to a large extent, the thrust of CE was tied up with issues of cost—if one could establish that certain procedures were clinically ineffective, this might provide a way of saving money.

"Promoting Clinical Effectiveness", 1996

In discussing the history of CE in the UK, Cape (2000) describes "Promoting Clinical Effectiveness" (NHS, 1996) as a more balanced document, considering the balance of cost versus CE. It outlines CE as a population based approach to quality improvement. It has the following components.

Evidence collection

- Research and Development: increasing our knowledge base about effectiveness and cost-effectiveness of care.

Dissemination and Implementation

Whatever state the knowledge base is in, the CE programme properly involves the following steps:

- Inform: this refers to sources of information i.e. the evidence base. The primary source of information is original research; however, the current emphasis is on effectiveness reviews— which synthesize evidence from research in a more digestible form. Another source is clinical guidelines, which collate evidence from research reviews and present it in a way to help clinicians make decisions. See Chapter Seven on "Evidence based practice" for more information on this.

- Change: this refers to methods for changing practice. These include CPD (continuing professional development), clinical audit and peer review.
- Monitor: this includes outcome monitoring which can be used as a local indicator, as well as for benchmarking of services and comparison with national results. Monitoring can also include comparing local audit results with national audits when there are national standards, as in the Patients' Charter (DOH, 1996).

"A First Class Service", 1998

By this stage, the CE agenda is no longer essentially about cost; it is now about quality, and making sure that care is clinically appropriate. A "First Class Service" DOH, 1998 outlines six stages necessary to achieve quality improvement. These are essentially a further development of the stages identified in "Promoting Clinical Effectiveness". They are:

- Identification: identify areas or issues which need to be considered for research into new technologies or for research into existing technologies/treatments
- Evidence collection: research to assess clinical and cost-effectiveness of interventions
- Appraisal and guidance: deciding from the evidence what would be useful in terms of guidance to the NHS in developing that kind of guidance
- Dissemination: disseminating guidance and supporting clinical audit
- Implementation: at a local level, through clinical governance
- Monitoring

At the core of "A First Class Service" is the concept of clinical governance. *Figure 2* (taken from "A First Class Service") sets out the structure of the document. It is clear from this that "clinical governance" has a key role in the quality programme and in delivering standards. The figure illustrates the key NHS structures that are intended to serve the quality improvement agenda.

Figure 2. The new NHS.

The National Institute for Clinical Excellence (NICE)

NICE is a special health authority, set up in April 1999, with new legislation developed in consultation with professional bodies. It is responsible for collating all the disparate material that exists in evidence based health care publications. It produces and disseminates clinical guidelines, clinical audit methodologies, and good practice information, as well as being responsible for running the National Confidential Enquiries, including those into suicides and homicides. See page 115 for more information.

The "National Service Frameworks for Mental Health"

National Service Frameworks (NSF) lay down the models of treatment and care to which people are entitled regardless of geographical location.

The "NSF for Mental Health" (DOH, 1999) is based on the White Paper "Modernising Mental Health Services". It focuses on the mental health needs of working age adults between the ages of 18 and 65, as well as the needs of children and young people when and where they come into contact with an adult with a mental illness, such as children living with a mentally ill parent. It sets standards in five areas:

1. Mental health promotion: to ensure that health and social services promote health and reduce the discrimination and social exclusion associated with mental health problems, with special attention to vulnerable groups, such as ethnic minorities, severe mentally ill, the homeless and prisoners.
2. Primary care and access to services: to deliver better primary health care and to ensure consistent advice and help for people with mental health needs, including primary care services for individuals with severe mental illness.
3. Effective services for people with severe mental illness: to ensure that each person with severe mental illness receives the range of mental health services they need; that crises are anticipated or prevented where possible; to ensure prompt and effective help if a crisis does occur; and timely access to an appropriate and safe inpatient treatment as close to home as possible.
4. Caring about carers: to ensure health and social services assess the needs of the carers who provide regular and substantial care for those with severe mental illness.
5. Preventing suicide: to ensure that health and social services play their part in achieving the target set in "Saving Lives, Our Healthier Nation" to reduce the suicide rate by at least one fifth by 2010.

The NSF for Mental Health concludes that, in order to meet these standards at organizational and professional levels, capability needs to increase, which will involve ever greater evidence of effectiveness.

This document is available on the Internet: www.doh.gov.uk/nsf/mentalhealth.htm

The Commission for Health Improvement (CHI)

This is an independent statutory body, the broad purpose of which is to improve patient care. CHI is supported by the Secretary of State for Health and the Director of Health Improvement. It conducts a rolling programme of Clinical Governance Reviews (CGRs) of Trusts focusing on the adequacy of clinical governance arrangements, implementation of the guidance produced by NICE and the implementation of the NSF. It has recently been subsumed by the Commission for Healthcare Audit and Inspection. For more information see Part IV. Information about CHI and CGRs are also available on the internet at: http://www.chi.nhs.uk/

Clinical Governance

Clinical Governance is clearly set out as the central part of the model for the "New NHS". It is described as a "framework for a local quality improvement programme". This framework includes quality improvement mechanisms, such as clinical audit and evidence based practice. However, the key principle of "clinical governance" is that responsibility for ensuring quality of services lies with the Chief Executive Officer of the Trust. A further emphasis of clinical governance is on involving everyone in quality improvement, including health professionals, academics, managers, patients, and the public. Generally, government documentation regarding any of these topics can be accessed at: www.doh.gov.uk/publications/index.html

The "NHS Plan" (2000)

The "NHS Plan" (DOH, 2000) defines the core principles of the NHS as a service that will:

1. Provide a service for all based on clinical need, not ability to pay.
2. Provide a comprehensive range of services.
3. Shape its services around the needs and preferences of individual patients, their families, and carers.
4. Respond to the differing needs in different populations.
5. Work to improve quality services and minimize errors.
6. Support and value its staff.
7. Public funds for health care will be devoted solely to NHS patients.
8. Work together with others to ensure a seamless service.
9. Help keep people healthy and work to reduce health inequalities
10. Respect confidentiality of individual patients and provide open access to information about services, treatment, and performance.

The "NHS Plan" shifts away from traditional forms of investment and strengthens the link between investment and reform. It blames the underperformance of the NHS on under funding, a lack of national standards, the maintenance of old fashioned demarcations between staff and services, a lack of incentives to improve performance and disempowered patients. It also attempts to redress the balance by linking funding to performance, greater workforce planning, by improving patient care and patient involvement and increasing the focus on crisis prevention and those who traditionally fall between the cracks, such as the elderly and the severely mentally ill.

References

Cape, J. (2000). Clinical Effectiveness in the UK: definitions, history and policy trends. *Journal of Mental Health*, 9(3): 237–246.

College Research Unit, Royal College of Psychiatrists, Clinical Effectiveness in Mental Health "99, Conference Abstracts,13/5/99.

Department of Health (1989). Working for Patients. NHS Executive.

Department of Health (1996a). Promoting Clinical Effectiveness. NHS Executive.

Department of Health (1996b). *The Patients' Charter*. London: HMSO.

Department of Health (1998). A First Class Service, Quality in the New NHS. NHS Executive.

Department of Health (1999). National Service Framework for Mental Health. NHS Executive.

Department of Health (2000). The NHS Plan—A plan for investment. A plan for reform. NHS Executive.

CHAPTER THREE

Case study of a mental health trust

T he Tavistock and Portman Clinics became an NHS Trust in 1994. They are NHS outpatient clinics providing a range of mental health services for psychological, emotional, and personality problems. Both clinics provide a range of services, which include family work, individual psychotherapy for children or adults, group therapy, and couple therapy. The Tavistock Clinic is also a training institution providing postgraduate mental health training.

Between "Working for Patients" and "A First Class Service", all UK Trusts had begun to employ staff for the purpose of quality improvement. By 1998 the typical make-up of a Clinical Audit Committee would, depending on the size of the Trust, involve one or two dedicated staff, e.g. a Clinical Audit Coordinator and/or Clinical Audit Assistant, and other staff dedicating one or two sessions to audit including: a clinical member of staff acting as Audit Lead in each department or speciality; a Trust Audit Chair (usually a senior clinician); and representatives from relevant staff groups, such as Junior Doctors, Specialist Registrars and the Health Authority. This structure, however, has undergone considerable transition in most Trusts (including the Tavistock and Portman

NHS Trust), particularly since 1998. These transitions reflect both the government agenda as well as the evolution of the concept of quality improvement from clinical audit alone to clinical effectiveness and evidence based practice among others. There are now many areas of the work of a Trust which involve quality improvement which now extend beyond the work of a Clinical Audit Committee.

The Committee structure of a Trust is not at best malleable. It is even less so when there is no clear impetus and framework for change as with "A First Class Service", which provided no clear imperatives for change regarding local structures. The transition process at the Tavistock and Portman NHS Trust is best described as a gradual evolution that was driven in part by individuals within the Trust and in part by the changing external environment and external requirements of the NHS.

In October 1998, the half-time audit assistant post was upgraded to a full-time Clinical Audit Facilitator post.

In April 1999, a Trust Audit Strategy for 1999/2000 was launched. The Strategy included the proposal that the Clinical Audit Committee develop its role more broadly into the domain of Clinical Effectiveness. During 1999, it became clear that the Committee had begun to address this wider role. The main priority identified for the Committee was the promotion of outcome monitoring projects. Several such projects began across the Trust and more were planned.

Another priority identified in the Strategy was raising the profile of clinical audit and effectiveness within the Trust. This became intertwined with the growing profile of clinical governance, which was partly driven by members of the Clinical Audit Committee who were more aware of the issues, and partly driven by increasing external requirements being placed on the Trust which were drawing in more and more individuals across the Trust's structures. A major landmark for the Trust was the "launch" of Clinical Governance in January 2000, which was a Trust-wide event with key speakers introducing the concept, together with some of its elements, and encouraging discussion. The event also marked the transition from a small group of four senior clinicians (including the Trust Audit Lead) working as a "governance group" on key tasks, to a Clinical Governance Committee responsible to the Trust Board. It was also at this point that the Clinical Audit Committee became the Clinical Audit and Effectiveness Committee—marking out clearly its broader role, including that of outcome monitoring.

By January 2000 with the "launch" of clinical governance, it was clear that the Clinical Audit Facilitator had become involved in many clinical governance related activities and the role was gradually turning into one of a Clinical Governance Support Officer. This included playing a key role in the formation of the User Involvement Committee and the Caldicott Group (addressing issues of confidentiality), as well as in the development of a new strategy for the Race and Equity Group. The evolution of the role into the new Clinical Governance Support Officer post was also made possible by the way in which the tasks of clinical audit had increasingly been devolved to clinical staff, so that projects only needed basic facilitation by the former Clinical Audit Facilitator. This was taken as a sign that quality improvement was gradually being adopted as part of the culture within departments, rather than as a separate activity carried out by the "audit person".

By the end of 2001, the Clinical Audit and Effectiveness working group was subsumed by the newly titled Clinical Governance & Quality Committee chaired by the Medical Director. In 2003, this committee needed two sub-committees which are responsible for the detailed working out of policy and for implementation in their respective areas: the Clinical Services Governance Sub-Committee and the Learning Strategy Sub-Committee. Several other Committees and working groups provide reports to the Clinical Governance Committees such as the Race and Equity Working Group, the User Involvement Committee, the Risk Management Group, the Care Programme Approach Working Party and the Caldicott Group. The Clinical Services Governance Sub-Committee initiates a variety of regular audits which include casenotes standards monitoring, GP communication and Care Programme Approach audits. It is responsible for the Trust's programme of outcome monitoring and liaises with the Trust's Information Technology Committee regarding the quantitative data required for Clinical Service monitoring. It reviews complaints and patient comment and feedback reports, and is establishing a better system for clinical incident monitoring. The Patient Survey is the responsibility of the Learning Strategy Sub-Committee. Its results are distributed widely. The Learning Strategy Sub-Committee is also responsible, with the Chair of the Professional

Committee, the Director of the Portman Clinic and the Heads of Discipline Group for Continuing Professional Development and appraisal processes.

Since the Clinical Audit Committee was set up in 1992, the evolving structures for first, clinical audit, and more recently clinical governance, have been organized to face towards, on the one hand, the Trust's management (the Trust board, the Management group and the Tavistock Professional Committee and the Portman Director) and, on the other, towards the departmental clinical leaderships, who actually provide the Trust's clinical services. Activity at these different levels has had a cumulative effect so that we now have, by and large, a group of clinicians and researchers who can work together effectively to deliver the different elements required of Clinical Governance and of the audit cycle. For instance, the repeated annual audits of casenotes, GP communication and Care Programme Approach, which have demonstrated significant improvements, are one evidence of the effective functioning of the system being built. The introduction of Care Programme Approach documentation and formal risk assessment has produced a sharper focus upon matters of risk assessment. The culture, and management style within the Trust continues to encourage clinician-led audit.

The Commission for Health Improvement's (CHI) review of the Trust started in September 2002. This involved complex preparation and a large amount of documentation, including a lengthy and detailed questionnaire about the Trust sent to CHI in November 2002. CHI employs a method of assessing a Trust by triangulating from different sources of information, including the opinion of stakeholders and of patients. The next stage of the review will involve interviews with patients in order to assess how patients view their treatment here. Throughout the review, staff at the Trust have been able to respond to the requirements of CHI and have supported each other well. The review culminates in a week-long visit beginning in January 2003. The final report, followed by an Action Plan is expected a few weeks later.

CHAPTER FOUR

Quality in psychological treatment services: reflections and developments

A udit is a tool which has a dual aim of monitoring, as well as improving, quality. As described already, it began to be adopted by the medical profession in experimental form during the 1970s. While the two activities of monitoring and improving are to a great extent integral to each other, they also provoke quite different feelings in those whose professional activities are the subject of the audit. Monitoring can feel persecutory, opening up the individual to potential criticism of their work and of their self. Improving quality, however, is an ideal which most professionals are keen to espouse as it has the potential to create a greater sense of pride in their work and themselves. This is the paradox of clinical audit and perhaps also the paradox of government involvement in the health service. By stamping an obligation on medical professionals to carry out audit, the government was in one sense demonstrating a firm will to improve the service for the sake of the public, but in another sense implying a lack of trust in the profession to take care of its own quality mechanisms.

To a certain extent, "quality" can be thought of as having become a pawn in a battle for public confidence in the health service. While both government and health professionals are no doubt committed to ensuring high quality services, the challenge is to persuade the public of this. In a sense the government's challenge is the greater as its lifespan is much shorter than a health professional's career and its survival is dependent on winning and maintaining public confidence. This may account for the bolder strategies that governments employ, involving the issuing of directives, imperatives, and programmes of reform. Meanwhile, the health care professional has multiple roles to perform, which include providing the best health care they can at the time, attempting to continually improve the quality of the care they provide, and conforming to any new government directives which may or may not contribute to improving the care they provide. Therefore, when considering whether to engage in or to resist taking part in activities arising from any new government agenda for health care, it is important to keep an open mind about whether the activity does have potential to improve care and whether any negative feelings of resistance towards the activity derive from genuine concern about the motives and aims of the activity or from a sense of threat and potential exposure, owing to the way in which the message is delivered rather than the actual content of the message.

Psychological treatment services are in a slightly different position, from that of the medical profession in general, where quality improvement is concerned. As with the medical profession, there are traditional means of ensuring quality of care, such as established methods of training, supervision, undertaking research, and conferences. There is little formal evidence establishing whether these traditional methods maintain and improve the quality of services compared with clinical audit and effectiveness programmes. However, much of the government agenda on quality has directed its new imperatives only to doctors, such as the obligation to participate in audit as set out in "Working for Patients". Only recently has the obligation to take part in audit and other quality improvement mechanisms spread to all health care professionals. To some extent this has allowed psychological treatment services an opportunity to experiment with and reflect on these activities with less of a sense of threat. This, perhaps coupled with the nature of the associated professions themselves, has resulted in a fairly reflective stance on clinical audit and other related activities by clinical psychology and related professions.

An example of this reflective stance is provided by the book *Rethinking Clinical Audit: The Case of Psychotherapy Services in the NHS* (Davenhill & Patrick, 1998) which tackles some of the difficult issues faced by psychotherapy services in introducing audit into their practice and reflects on some of the ways in which practitioners react to clinical audit. The following extract illustrates an attempt to interpret audit activity and practitioners' reactions to this activity drawing on psychoanalytic and Kleinian theories:

> One aspect of the process of clinical audit involves a critical scrutiny of what is taking place. This includes a spectrum of behaviour ranging from listening, to hearing, to perceiving, to noting, to observing, to looking, to inspecting, to examining and to exploring. Again, there are major familial, social and cultural attitudes that govern our ability to look at and observe what may be going on.
>
> Eye contact, for example, can have differing meanings in different societies related to social and sexual roles. It may also have particular personal intra-psychic meanings for a particular individual. Being able to look and take in with the eyes what is actually happening in the world around one is a feature of what Melanie Klein termed "depressive position functioning" (Segal, 1973), and what Donald Winnicott (1965) called "a capacity for concern". In this position people and things are permitted to be what they are, and not transformed into the fearful ogres or idolised figures so characteristic of a more primitive and paranoid way of perceiving the world. In other instances, looking may be understood as an active attacking process. We are all familiar with the phrase "if looks could kill" and with the concept of a "penetrating stare" or, when feeling guilty, of not being able to look someone in the eye or face. This form of looking would seem more directly connected with the internal world of the looker, and may be more closely associated with less mature levels of psychological functioning. [Davenhill & Patrick, 1998]

Clinical audit involves evaluating practice against pre-set standards. While standards can be derived from various areas, such as ethics, consumer demands, and so on, they ought largely to be derived from good quality research evidence indicating what best practice is in terms of outcomes and cost. Therefore, although clinical audit has been tackled seriously by those working in psychological treatment services, there exists a certain paradox in the way that it was the first quality-related activity to be promoted by the government, before clinical and cost-effectiveness and evidence based practice. Although true to a certain extent for all areas of health care, it is particularly true of psychological treatment services that only limited evidence exists about best practice.

In 1996 the Department of Health undertook a NHS Review of Psychotherapy Services in England (Parry & Richardson, 1996). This indicated a growing demand in the NHS for psychological therapies. As part of this, the NHS commissioned a research review, which collated for the first time in this country the evidence for the effectiveness of psychological treatments (Roth & Fonagy, 1996). Together these two documents offer practical guidance to purchasers, providers, employers, and trainers about how to drive forward the agenda of evidence based practice in psychotherapy and how to improve the quality of existing services. However, while signalling the benefits of psychotherapy in general terms, the Review also pointed to the dearth of available evidence for the effectiveness of the psychoanalytic psychotherapies, especially where controlled trials were concerned. Although a number of recently published studies have started to fill this gap, there is much work still to do. For this reason the Tavistock and Portman NHS Trust has set up a new Psychotherapy Evaluation Research Unit (PERU), with a view to collecting the evidence needed concerning both the efficacy and the effectiveness of its therapeutic methods (primarily psycho-analytic and systemic in nature), including where appropriate, carrying out substantial randomized controlled trials. In Chapters Five and Six, Phil Richardson and Peter Hobson present some of the complex considerations relating to the evidence available for NHS psychotherapy and Arlene Vetere presents a summary of the evidence available on the effectiveness of marital, family and systemic therapies.

The 1996 Review of Psychotherapy Services was produced in the same year as the document "Promoting Clinical Effectiveness" (DOH, 1996a) described earlier. While the core elements of the latter (inform, change, and monitor) are as applicable to psychological treatment services as to other domains of health care, in practice their application is problematic in that the knowledge base upon which the "inform" stage might rely is deficient, as described above. Nevertheless, given that there is some evidence, psychological treatment services have attempted to employ the mechanisms for promoting clinical effectiveness as set out in the document. The function of informing practice has been characterized in many domains by the proliferation of clinical practice guidelines which draw together the available evidence concerning the most effective treatments for different conditions. Psychological Treatment Services have not shied away from this challenge and the DOH has recently published the National Psychological Therapies and Counselling Referral Guideline (Parry, 2001), which is available for use by GPs and other primary health care practitioners. Guidelines are controversial however, and commonly become erroneously identified with prescriptive approaches to practice. This guideline and other issues relating to guidelines are discussed further in Part IV.

Change and monitoring also occur in psychological treatment services through mechanisms such as local clinical audit, described in more detail in Part II, as well as national audits, such as the national Child and Adolescent Mental Health Services audit (Audit Commission, 1999). Routine data collection and outcome monitoring is also fairly standard now in services, again not without controversy where psychological treatments are concerned. This is discussed in Chapter Five by Phil Richardson on RCTs and evidence based practice in psychodynamic psychotherapies. The Chapter includes discussion of the three main problems of applying such principles to psychological treatment services: firstly, what constitutes evidence elsewhere in health care might not be equally applicable to these fields; secondly, the criteria we use to assess the quality of evidence may vary according to the domain of enquiry, such that a good psychotherapy outcome study may have different features from a good drug trial; and thirdly, and relatedly, the research methods which are considered of highest value in the hierarchy of treatment evaluation research elsewhere, notably randomized controlled trials, may be particularly problematic where psychoanalytic or systemic psychotherapy is concerned). Details of specific approaches to outcome monitoring in psychological treatment services are also discussed in Part III.

References

Audit Commission (1999). Children in mind: child and adolescent mental health services (national report). London: Audit Commission Publications.

Davenhill, R., & Patrick, M. (Eds) (1998). *Rethinking Clinical Audit*. London: Routledge.

Parry, G. (2000). Treatment choice guidelines in psychotherapy. *Journal of Mental Health*, 9(3): 273–281.

Roth, A., & Fonagy, P. (1996). *What Works for Whom? A Critical Review of Psychotherapy Research*. New York: Guilford.

CHAPTER FIVE

In defence of NHS psychotherapy

P. H. Richardson and R. P. Hobson

Abstract—This paper takes the form of an imagined conversation between a sceptical interviewer and a psychotherapist from the Tavistock Clinic. The focus of the conversation is whether it is justifiable to practice psychodynamic and systemic psychotherapy in the NHS. Our aim is to explore some (just some) of the options one has in responding to a cross-examination of this kind. We limit the factual content (and in particular, the research evidence cited) so that the interested reader may feel armed but not overburdened.

Introduction

Sooner or later, most psychoanalytic psychotherapists are challenged to justify their work. This may be a relatively relaxed experience, say during a dinner-party, or it may become as a harrowing onslaught from other professionals, managers, or politicians. It can be very difficult to find mental space to think under such circumstances. When an interrogation takes the form of demands for evidence, one may wish one had more facts at one's disposal. Our intention in this paper is to illustrate how we might confidently respond to enquiries about our work, drawing on some but not many pieces of factual evidence. In order to take up different perspectives before citing the evidence itself (a little of which—say, three references—may be worth reading and remembering in detail), we leave our brief summary of some useful research until the end.

We should explain why the interview takes a particular slant, and specifically a Tavistock viewpoint. The reason is that the services of the Tavistock Clinic in London have recently come under public scrutiny through the broadcasting of a six-part BBC2 TV series entitled 'Talking Cure'. Much of the work of the clinic is psychotherapeutic, with a particular emphasis on psychoanalytic and systemic models of change. The broadcasting of our clinical work has prompted a number of invitations to media events, and we anticipated that these interviews might involve questions about the efficacy, effectiveness, and cost-effectiveness of psychodynamic therapy. Therefore in a spirit of self-scrutiny, a number of senior clinicians met to consider just how our forms of psychotherapy square up to the challenges of evidence-based practice and, in particular, where they stand in a potentially competitive therapeutic marketplace.

The imaginary interview reported below represents a distillation of some of the thinking that emerged during this exercise. We offer it to colleagues who may be struggling with similar concerns about the standing of their methods in the context of our common endeavour to provide clinically effective services. We appreciate that much of the interview might be described as Tavisto-centric, but assume that colleagues elsewhere will be able to extrapolate or adjust the arguments, where it is appropriate to do so, to their own local situation.

Domains of questioning are shown **in bold**; imaginary interviewer questions are shown *in italics*.

Evidence of benefits from psychotherapy

Where is the evidence for the benefits of your therapy?

The evidence is of different kinds. For example, those who have seen the Talking Cure series may be able to judge for themselves whether the Tavistock's approach to the people depicted was appropriate, sensitive, and emotionally authentic. There are real benefits to be gained from taking very seriously and listening in detail to people's worries and mental pain, and in trying to make sense of what people find overwhelming and unmanageable. It is an approach that helps people to help themselves; and it is a very different approach to classifying their problems as, for example, 'depressive disorder' or 'anxiety state', and treating it with medication or techniques to change behaviour or abnormal thinking. So there is the kind of evidence that is available for the judgment of the layperson. The point about psychotherapy is that it links with common-sense, how most people understand what makes human beings tick, but it then goes beyond common sense to areas that most people cannot understand nor help.

Then there is evidence from the experience of clinicians, who have a view of the background of emotional problems and have seen how psychotherapy helps people to deal with their feelings and relationships in new and less distressing ways. They see how people *develop* through a psychotherapeutic relationship, whether in individual, group, or family therapy.

Then there is evidence from published reports of treated cases, which provide more formal and detailed accounts of such changes.

Then there is evidence from research in developmental psychology, which shows that children's ways of relating to others, their self-esteem and their confidence at school is connected with the sensitivity with which their caregivers have responded to them. This gives an indication of the power of relationships to transform personal experience. Moreover, recent research indicates that at least some emotional disorders in adults have close links to patterns of attachment—and psychotherapy is best suited to changing these patterns.

Then we move to the more formal kinds of study, including what are called Randomised Controlled Trials. Some researchers consider these to be the only real evidence, but that is a very narrow view. Such trials depend on treating forms of psychological distress as medical conditions—and that is sometimes justified—and treating psychotherapy as if it were like a kind of medication or surgery. So these studies have an important place in evaluating psychotherapy from a particular point of view (treating 'conditions' rather than individuals, with standardised rather than more individually tailored treatments). Psychotherapists are now producing evidence that, even when these simplifications are made, psychotherapy is effective for a number of hard-to-treat 'conditions' such as alcohol dependence, depression in the elderly, and forms of chronic emotional and relationship difficulties ('personality disorders').

The important thing to recognise is that any given kind of evidence has its strengths and weaknesses—and it is the overall picture (unrecognised by many critics) that is so persuasive.

Clinical expertise alone is no basis for practice

You say that you have a wealth of evidence for the benefits of your treatment methods, including that which comes from the wisdom and expert judgment of highly experienced clinicians. Do you think that the parents of the Bristol heart case children who died would be satisfied with that kind of answer; don't you think that the Bristol case doctors might have called upon their own lengthy clinical experience to justify their practices? Is it not precisely because of the frequent failure of clinical judgment that modern medicine and health care now take an 'evidence-based' approach?

My response follows from what I have just said about the strengths and weaknesses of any given approach. I have emphasised that the Tavistock Clinic strongly endorses the evidence-based approach as one important perspective. This should not blind us, however, to the realities. What we must also remember is that the great majority of medical treatments, not just in psychiatry, have a long way to go before they can be practised in a fully evidence based way. There is so much more evidence that needs collecting, and psychotherapists are carrying out careful research on our treatment methods.

We must also be careful not to throw the baby out with the bathwater. Having the right evidence to guide what you do as a clinician is clearly very important. This does not mean that clinical judgment can be dispensed with. Scientific evidence can tell you about what works for the **average** or typical patient—the textbook case. Doctors and psychotherapists will always have to call on their clinical judgment for the treatment of the **individual** case—however much the evidence may tell us about the **average** case. In psychotherapy we believe that everyone is an individual—the concept of the average patient doesn't make much sense.

You need randomised trial evidence

According to Professor ... a leading authority on evidence based medicine the only scientifically persuasive evidence for the effectiveness of a treatment is a positive result from a so-called 'randomised trial'. We have been given to believe that there is not a single published randomised trial demonstrating the effectiveness of your kind of therapy with working age adults. Can this really be true?

No, it is not true. But first let us agree that randomised trials provide a powerful source of evidence for the effectiveness of treatments, which is why we have a programme of research at the Tavistock based on these methods. What the experts also agree on is that they do not provide the only source of evidence. Nor are they foolproof: The conditions in which randomised trials are carried out are often highly atypical of everyday clinical practice, and the patients who are included in these trials are highly selected and not at all typical of a great many of the 'multi-problem' patients who seek psychotherapy in the NHS. We simply don't know how far the results of most randomised trials can truly be applied in the 'real world' of NHS patients with everyday mental health problems. This difficulty is found to some extent in all areas of medicine but is also a particular problem in psychotherapy.

In fact there is now a growing body of evidence from randomised trials currently appearing in scientific journals that psychoanalytic and systemic psychotherapy methods are efficacious with a variety of problems including depression, alcoholism, personality disorder and so on (see below).

But there is still so little evidence

(Well you have referred to a sprinkling of recent studies here, but ...) ... is it not true that science proceeds by accumulating a substantial body of evidence from repeated investigations of the same question. These are called replication studies. Have any of the studies you refer to been replicated—or repeated in this way?

Yes, the results from these studies accord with previous published research reports. What is important about the new (randomised trial) results is that they are showing that earlier suggestive findings hold up well to the most rigorous kind of scientific scrutiny.

Other treatments already have so much evidence

Other treatments have a long history of obtaining evidence in scientifically rigorous ways. How can you justify going on trying to prove that your methods work when there is already so much more evidence for the effectiveness of other treatments like cognitive therapy? Shouldn't the health service simply recommend that cognitive therapy become the treatment of choice where psychotherapy is concerned? (Variant: And/or invest exclusively in improving CBT methods and plugging the gaps in the CBT evidence base?)

It is true that CBT has produced some evidence of benefit, but one must not overestimate the quality and depth of that evidence. In reality, the research too is very limited, for example insofar as atypical cases are selected for treatment, the length of follow-up is short, and it employs a narrow view of what it means for a treatment to 'work'. It does not address many of the things we covered earlier, such as the way people develop and change through making sense of their patterns of relationship.

It is important not to forget that psychotherapy is not like surgery. One day it may be proved that for any particular medical problem there is a single surgical operation, or other treatment, that works best for all patients. Psychotherapy is different. The **patient** has to work in psychotherapy too, not just the doctor. So the patient has to have a therapy that suits him/her as an **individual**. For this reason it is likely that there will always need to be different therapies to meet the needs of different patients. Research and experience have shown us that in psychotherapy the patient's attitude to treatment is an important influence on whether he or she can use the treatment effectively.

Secondly, whilst it is true that some treatments have more evidence for their usefulness from randomised trials this shouldn't blind us to the fact that much of that evidence has been collected on a very narrow group of patients who are not typical of NHS referrals. For example the major studies which prove that cognitive therapy helps people with depression were carried out on patients whose problems were far less extensive and long-standing than most of those who are typically referred to psychotherapy departments.

This last point might seem like quibbling until you consider that one of the latest major treatment studies, which did try to treat people with long-standing and complex problems of depression, found that it was necessary to give up trying to use cognitive therapy with this group of patients (Leff et al, 2000). Patients offered cognitive therapy were dropping out of the study and the therapists considered them too 'atypical' to treat. These are the patients we treat every day. The same study found that the methods we use at the Tavistock were highly effective, and for some symptoms more so than drug treatment.

Briefer treatments work fine. Why bother with yours?

We understand that your therapy commonly takes at least a year to complete, and sometimes takes much longer. Given that there is now a wealth of good scientific evidence that much briefer treatments can be highly effective with a wide range of everyday psychological problems, like depression and anxiety, can you really justify carrying on with your much more expensive methods (for which moreover there is very limited scientific proof of effectiveness)?

Of course we need to think about how cost-effective our treatments are. We also need to keep one or two other things in mind too:

Firstly we must also remember that a treatment that is not effective can't possibly be cost-effective—however cheap it is. Where the severe and complex and enduring mental health problems are concerned, all the therapies (including cognitive therapy) are in a similar boat: that is to say that, although we have some very encouraging findings on our treatments, we don't yet know enough about their clinical effectiveness. And so we must go on collecting the relevant evidence.

This is especially true of the long-term effects of therapy. Once again **most** therapies (including CBT) are in the same boat—in that we don't know enough yet about how long their benefits can be expected to last. Perhaps later I can describe some recent evidence that demonstrates how, at least in the treatment of certain conditions, a remarkable feature of psychodynamic psychotherapy is the way in which it promotes continuing and progressive improvement even after the treatment has ended.

So, whilst we are aware of the importance of working cost-effectively, we are also aware that we need to be careful not to become too enamoured of quick fix therapies. We believe that there are few quick fixes for the kinds of problems that are serious enough to be referred to us.

Having said this it is worth mentioning that a number of recently conducted studies have provided impressive estimates of the benefits of our methods in reducing hospitalisation, medication, GP consultations, etc (eg Guthrie et al 1999, Stevenson and Meares, 1992—see below).

You treat the worried well

You say that for more severe mental heath problems your therapy may be justified because it may be more effective than the shorter treatments. Do you see people suffering from schizophrenia in your clinic?

Not usually. We are an outpatient clinic and it is sometimes necessary to admit people with schizophrenia for an inpatient stay. We don't have the facilities to treat this group of patients at the time of an acute breakdown. What we can offer is follow-up therapy to individuals who have previously suffered such a breakdown and who now understand that there may be more to dealing with their difficulties than relying exclusively on long-term medication. In addition we do a great deal of work in helping the carers of the seriously ill—whether in the caring professions, or in families.

*I see ... so what you're saying is that it's **not** the really severe mental health problems that you treat. In fact it has been suggested that the majority of patients that you see have relatively minor problems and might be described as the 'worried well of Hampstead'. What would you say to that?*

Firstly we should clear up any misconception that the Tavistock only treats patients from the narrow geographical area where it is located. We see people from a very wide area across London and beyond. In fact we recently commissioned an independent expert from another university (Professor Spence from University of Warwick) to analyse where our patients typically come from. What emerged from this very careful analysis was that the vast preponderance (4 out of 5) of our patients come from the most deprived and socially disadvantaged areas of London.

Moreover a substantial number of our patients come with very serious problems including histories of violence, self-harm and suicide attempts, as well as severe depression and other mental illnesses—so the 'worried well' idea is clearly a myth.

Few patients can access and benefit from your therapy

Psychoanalytic therapy has been criticised for being available only to a highly selected group of rather privileged (intelligent, well educated, etc) patients. Perhaps you could tell us how many of the patients referred to your clinic actually end up in therapy, and how many are described as unsuitable and sent back to their GPs?

Yes, we're aware of this sort of comment, which seems to be a bit of a hangover from the time—at the turn of the century—when Freud treated mainly the Viennese middle classes. In fact it no longer has any basis in reality. The majority of people who do not get seen after being referred to the Tavistock are simply those who do not attend for the appointments they have been sent. It is rare for a patient not to be seen once they have been referred.

Moreover there is no evidence that we know of, that our therapeutic approaches are less effective or useful with less intelligent or less well educated people. Indeed one of our specialist services offers psychotherapeutic help to people with learning disabilities.

Other treatments are better for serious problems

Another follow on from worried well idea ...
I see, so some of your patients do have fairly serious problems involving self harm, suicide attempts etc, and these are the ones that you claim to be able to help better with your longer term treatments. Isn't it true, however, that the only solid evidence here shows that it is a form of cognitive-

behavioural therapy which can reduce suicide attempts in people with these severe problems? Are you able to prove, in this way, that your therapy works with these people?

It is true that we need more evidence in this area—though this applies to all therapies. The evidence we do have for the benefits of psychoanalytic approaches is highly encouraging and on a par with the CBT evidence. As well as early research showing that a high proportion of such patients treated with our methods make substantial improvements (eg Stevenson and Meares, 1992) we now have randomised trials which convey the same message (Bateman and Fonagy, 1999; Guthrie et al 1999)

Can you justify long term/intensive therapy on the NHS?

Is it true that some patients might be seen at the Tavistock for as many as three times a week and for as long as three years?

Yes.

How can you justify this?

We are still learning about the benefits of intensive therapy. We believe that certain problems may only be helped with a longer-term approach, and that the longer-term effects of intensive therapy are likely to be greater. There are indications from high quality research that this may be so. In one study in Stockholm, patients in intensive treatment showed greater improvements some years after the therapy stopped than patients in less intensive therapy—even though the patient groups, intensive and non-intensively treated, appeared to be doing the same at the end of treatment (Sandell et al, 1999).

I calculate that one patient being seen three times a week for 3 years consumes as much therapist time as nine patients in once weekly psychotherapy for a year (which is already hardly a brief treatment in terms of other therapies). How can you justify this in a service where demand is almost always going to exceed supply—with the NHS chronically short of cash as it is?

We believe we can justify this in the case of a small minority of patients (for this is all that is involved) who effectively constitute special cases. We need to ask whether there are potential long-term benefits **and** cost savings for people who, without intensive therapy, might not be helpable at all. Our initial observations indicate that patients in intensive therapy are also much less likely to make their usual heavy demands on their general practitioners. We recognise, however, that further research is needed on these questions. This is currently under way in separate studies in Germany, Sweden and Finland and we are planning to follow suit with our own programme of research.

The Tavistock Clinic is also a major NHS training base for psychotherapy, and it is the opinion of many experienced trainers that we need to train advanced therapists using these intensive treatment methods—in order to enable them to do briefer and less intensive therapy in the most effective and efficient way. This is also an important area for future research.

Variant: Since long term treatment, like Viagra, is so costly can it in any case be justified in a financially hard pressed NHS where people are dying for lack of a sufficiently speedy or affordable transplant or other lifesaving treatment?

This is not a question about research! Readers must find their own answer.

Race and equity issues—ethnic minority groups can't get therapy

It is commonly claimed that ethnic minority groups have very little chance of receiving your kind of therapy? Can this really be true in this day and age?

Yes. We know that, for people from ethnic minorities with mental health problems, access to psychotherapy is poor, though we should emphasise that this is true across the board (ie for all kinds of psychological therapy, not just those which we practice). At the Tavistock we have a special group working on ways of improving access. A problem is that much depends on the referrers (ie on what happens before they get to us). We have to get to the GPs and others in the community. With this in mind we have a special Bangladeshi project team working with schools, local GPs and other community settings etc to improve access to services by the Asian community.

All right, so tell me about some evidence of a 'scientific' kind!

Let me do that in three ways.

(a) Firstly, let us take a general view, and consider studies that take a mix of conditions like anxiety, depression, and so on. There are scientific reviews that assess a number of studies together. One that was published in 1992 (Crits-Christoph) looked at 11 studies of brief dynamic psychotherapy, and concluded that in terms of target symptoms, general symptoms and social adjustment, the average patient receiving brief dynamic therapy was better off than 80% of the patients who were on waiting lists.

Or again, a leading researcher called Piper and colleagues have recently reported that interpretative therapy led from disordered to relatively normal functioning (clinical cut-off criteria) in over 50% of cases of depression, over 25% of those with anxiety, and almost 60% of those with significant psychiatric symptomatology on a standard measure (SCL-90) (Piper et al, 1998).

Or yet again, a recent study by Guthrie, Margison and colleagues in Manchester has demonstrated that brief psychodynamic therapy is effective not only in reducing symptoms and improving social functioning, but also in reducing health utilisation in the 6 months after intervention. It is an approach that saves money! About half of the treated group but about one sixth of the control patients (who received usual out-patient treatment, sometimes including antidepressant and behavioural treatments) showed clinical improvement (Guthrie et al 1999).

(b) Secondly, let us focus on an especially hard-to-treat group, patients who have what are sometimes known as personality disorders—with abrupt changes in mood, unstable relationships, often self-harming behaviour, and other serious difficulties.

In a study of 30 patients with 'borderline personality disorder' who had one year of twice-weekly out-patient psychotherapy, the patients' functioning one year before treatment was compared with the year after treatment. On all 7 objective behavioural indicators, including visits to the doctor, drug taking, violent behaviour, self-harm, hospital admission and psychiatric symptoms (DSM III), the patients had improved, and one third could no longer be considered to fall into the category of this personality disorder (Stevenson and Meares, 1992).

One can criticise that study because it was not controlled (although it is still convincing, because it is implausible that this group would have changed so much spontaneously), but then we have the study from the Henderson (Dolan et al, 1997), looking at about 70 patients with severe personality disorder who received in-patient treatment and 70 who did not. The treated group showed a greater reduction on a self-report Borderline Syndrome Index than did the untreated group; indeed, over 40% of the treated group showed reliable and clinically significant improvement, but fewer than 20% of untreated patients. Moreover, improvement was related to length of treatment.

And in a third setting—a day hospital treatment based on psychoanalytic principles—Bateman and Fonagy (1999) have con-ducted a Randomised Controlled Trial comparing this approach with routine treatment. The results were that the group treated on psychoanalytic principles showed greater reduction in depression, self-harm and hospitalisation. These trials can be connected with other evidence that psychodynamic approaches are relevant and important in understanding the nature and treatment of such troubled patients: at the Tavistock, Hobson, Patrick and colleagues have shown how patients with borderline personality disorder have characteristic ways of experiencing and relating to other people, and also characteristic problems with organising their thoughts, feelings and memories about significant relationships—and it is precisely such abnormalities that psychotherapy addresses (Hobson et al 1998).

A more recent randomised trial, the Trondheim Psychotherapy Study of the treatment of Cluster C personality disorders, found evidence for continued improvement in patients treated with short term dynamic therapy up to two years following the end of treatment—an effect not found in the patients treated by cognitive therapy in the same study (Svartberg, 1999).

(c) Thirdly, we may consider other conditions that are very difficult to treat. Here are two examples.

The London Intervention Study (also mentioned above) showed that a brief systemic/dynamic therapy for couples was every bit as effective as antidepressant medication in the short term for chronic and complex cases of depression, and at follow-up proved to be more effective on some measures (Leff et al, 2000). You may recall that in this study, cognitive therapy failed to leave the starting blocks. This challenges the idea that an evidence-based approach to the treatment of depression can rely exclusively on drug treatments and cognitive therapy.

A recently published study by Sandahl et al (1998) demonstrated that psychodynamic group therapy could be effective in reducing alcohol intake in alcohol-dependent patients. This is a population for whom it is often thought that psychodynamic approaches are inappropriate. In this randomised trial there was a significantly greater improvement in patients receiving group therapy than those receiving CBT, as judged by abstinence at 15 month follow-up. This represents a substantial therapeutic achievement with alcohol-dependent patients according to a 'hard' measure of outcome.

We can see that the world has moved on considerably in the last three or four years. New studies on our treatment methods are appearing at an impressive rate—witness the overview recently produced by Peter Fonagy and Colleagues from the Research Committee of the International Psychoanalytic Association (Fonagy et al 1999).

Mmm ... your case seems surprisingly convincing.
All a bit disconcerting ...

References

Bateman, A., and Fonagy, P. (1999) The effectiveness of partial hospitalization in the treatment of borderline personality disorder—a randomised controlled trial. *American Journal of Psychiatry* **156**: 1563–1569

Crits-Christoph, P. (1992). The efficacy of brief dynamic psychotherapy: A meta-analysis. *American Journal of Psychiatry*, 149, 151–158.

Dolan, B., Warren, F and Norton, K. (1997). Change in borderline symptoms one year after therapeutic community treatment for severe personality disorder. *British Journal of Psychiatry*, 171, 274–279.

Fonagy, P., Kachele, R., Jones, E., and Perron, R. (1999). *An open-door review of outcome studies in psychoanalysis: Report prepared by the Research Committee of the IPA*. Available at http://www.ipa.org.uk/R-outcome.htm

Guthrie, E; Moorey, J; Margison, F; Barker, H; Palmer, S; McGrath, G; Tomenson, B; Creed, F (1999), Cost-effectiveness of brief psychodynamic-interpersonal therapy in high utilizers of psychiatric services, *Archives of General Psychiatry*, 56, 519–526

Hobson, R.P., Patrick, M.P.M., and Valentine, J.D. (1998). Objectivity in psychoanalytic judgements. *British Journal of Psychiatry*, 173, 172–177.

Leff, J., Vearnals, S., Brewin, C., et al (2000). The London Intervention Trial: an RCT of anti-depressants vs couple therapy in the treatment and maintenance of depressed people with a partner: Clinical outcome and cost. *British Journal of Psychiatry*. 177. 95–100

Piper, W.E., Joyce, A.S., McCallum, M., and Azim, H.A. (1998). Interpretive and supportive forms of psychotherapy and patient personality variables. *Journal of Consulting and Clinical Psychology*, 66, 558–567.

Sandahl, C, et al (1998). Time-limited group psychotherapy for moderately alcohol dependent patients: a randomised controlled trial. *Psychotherapy Research*, 8, 4 361–78.

Sandell R, Blomberg J and Lazar A (1999). Multimodal analysis of temporal interactions in the effects of psychoanalysis and long-term psychotherapy. Invited paper at the Conference: 'Psychoanalytische Langzeitbehandlungen. Eine Herausforderung fur clinische und empirische Forscher.' Hamburg, Germany. October 1999

Stevenson, J, and Meares, R. (1992). An outcome study of psychotherapy for patients with borderline personality disorder. *American Journal of Psychiatry*, 149, 358–62

Svartberg M and Stiles T (1999). The Trondheim Psychotherapy Study: A randomised trial of short term dynamic therapy vs cognitive therapy for Cluster C personality disorder. Paper presented to the Thirtieth International Conference of the Society for Psychotherapy Research, Braga, Portugal, June, 1999

CHAPTER SIX

On the effectiveness of family, marital and systemic therapies[1]

Arlene Vetere

T he practice of couples and family therapists rests on a growing empirical base of outcome evidence, drawn from studies of therapeutic efficacy and effectiveness. According to Bergin and Garfield (1994), the marital and family therapy approaches have been subjected to rigorous scrutiny, with only a few other forms of psychotherapy so frequently studied Studies report the use of controlled and uncontrolled group comparison designs, single case designs, and studies comparing the relative efficacy of the different family therapy approaches. The overwhelming findings from the research reviews and meta-analytic studies is that family therapy works compared to untreated control groups, with some demonstrated superiority to standard and individual treatments for certain disorders and populations (Pinsof & Wynne, 1995; Carr, 2000a,b). Meta-analysis demonstrates moderate, statistically significant and often clinically significant effects (Shadish *et al.*, 1995). The research literature supporting this conclusion is at least as robust as it is for other modes of psychotherapy.

The major review studies and their findings

The early studies of the outcome of marital and family therapy were reviewed by Gurman *et al.*, 1986. Their conclusions included the following:

a) non-behavioural marital and family therapies produce beneficial outcomes in about two-thirds of cases, and their effects are superior to no treatment;

b) when both spouses/partners are involved in therapy conjointly in the face of marital problems, there is a greater chance of positive outcome than when only one spouse is treated;

c) the developmental level of the "identified patient" (e.g. child, adolescent, adult) does not affect treatment outcomes significantly;

d) positive results of both non-behavioural and behavioural marital and family therapies typically occur in treatments of short duration i.e. 1–20 sessions; and

e) family therapy is as effective as and possibly more effective than many commonly offered (usually individual) treatments for problems attributed to family conflict.

Meta-analyses of outcome studies

The following meta-analytic reviews document a growing body of evidence that shows that the couples and family therapies work: Hazelrigg *et al.* (1987); Markus *et al.* (1990); Shadish *et al.* (1995); and Goldstein and Miklowitz (1995). The following list of people and problems is found to benefit both clinically and significantly from the marital and family therapies compared to no psychotherapy: marital/couple distress and conflict; outpatient depressed women in distressed marriages; adult drinking problems and drug misuse; adult schizophrenia; adolescent conduct disorder; anorexia in young adolescent girls; adolescent drug misuse; child conduct disorders; aggression and non-compliance in children with a diagnosis of ADHD; chronic physical illnesses in children, obesity in children and cardiovascular risk factors in children. Roth and Fonagy (1996) further reviewed the above studies in their attempt to map the evidence for the demonstrated efficacy of the psychotherapies in controlled research conditions and clinical effectiveness in services as delivered.

Couples and family therapy appears not to be harmful, in that no RCT study has reported poorer outcomes for treated clients than for untreated control family members (Pinsof & Wynne, 1995).

Family therapy as part of multi-component and integrative approaches

Chamberlain and Rosicky (1995), in their review of family intervention studies for severe adolescent conduct disorder and delinquency, found that family therapy approaches appeared to decrease adolescent conduct problems and delinquent behaviour compared to individual treatment and no treatment. However, they noted that when treatment failure or "dropout" occurred, it correlated highly with poverty and/or social isolation for the family. The Florida Network Study (Nugent et al., 1993), with high risk families, found that families who received family therapy were four times as likely to stay together as families who did not, and families who received more than five treatment sessions were twice as likely to stay together as families who did not. So, for these high risk families, family therapy may be a necessary treatment component, but is not sufficient in itself. When working therapeutically with severe problems, such as schizophrenia and adolescent conduct disorder, there is increasing evidence of the value of treatment packages, of which family therapy is a part (Pinsof & Wynne, 1995).

Cost-effectiveness of the family therapies

The cost-effectiveness advantages of family based interventions for some problems are beginning to emerge from a few studies. For example, there are preliminary data indicating that family therapy is more effective that alternative treatments for adult alcohol problems and adult and adolescent drug misuse. In addition, family therapy seems to be more cost-effective that standard inpatient/residential treatment for schizophrenia and severe adolescent conduct disorders and delinquency (Pinsof & Wynne, 1995).

Law and Crane's (2000) audit study showed that visits by family members to primary health care practitioners were significantly reduced following family therapy intervention.

Methodological problems

Methodological and conceptual problems beset the conduct of outcome studies in the field. These include: (a) the need for clearer definition of the presenting problem and the level of severity; (b) tighter control for attention–placebo effects in the comparison conditions; (c) couples and family therapies need to be more empirically described and verified with more process checks made for therapist activity; (d) studies need to include larger numbers of participants; and (e) more studies need to include the evaluation of outcome at multiple levels, consistent with systemic thinking (Pinsof & Wynne, 1995). The third generation of outcome researchers have turned their attention to these knotty problems, whose solutions will benefit the field of psychotherapy outcome research in general. For example, the London Intervention Depression Trial (Leff *et al.*, 2000), an RCT study of antidepressants versus systemic couples therapy in the treatment and maintenance of depressed people with a partner, used a manual for the couples therapy and specified the treatment length within circumscribed goals of the study. The study demonstrated the effectiveness of systemic couples therapy for moderate to severe depression.

Note

1. The outcome literature commonly reviews together studies of the efficacy of both couples therapies and the family therapies.

References

Bergin, A., & Garfield, S. (Eds) (1994). *Handbook of Psychotherapy and Behavior Change* (4th edn). New York: Wiley.

Carr, A. (2000a). Evidence-based practice in family therapy and systemic consultation I. *Journal of Family Therapy*, 22, 29–60.

Carr, A. (2000b). Evidence-based practice in family therapy and systemic consultation II. *Journal of Family Therapy, 22,* 273–295.

Chamberlain, P., & Rosicky, J. (1995). The effectiveness of family therapy in the treatment of adolescents with conduct disorders and delinquency. *Journal of Marital and Family Therapy, 21,* 441–459.

Goldstein, M., & Miklowitz, D. (1995). The effectiveness of psycho-educational family therapy in the treatment of schizophrenic disorders. *Journal of Marital and Family Therapy, 21,* 361–376.

Gurman, A., Kniskern, D., & Pinsof, W. (1986). Research on the process and outcome of marital and family therapy. In: S. Garfield & A. Bergin (Eds), *Handbook of Psychotherapy and Behavior Change* (3rd edn). New York: Wiley.

Hazelrigg, M., Cooper, H., & Borduin, C. (1987). Evaluating the effectiveness of family therapies: an integrative review and analysis. *Psychological Bulletin, 101,* 428–442.

Law, D., & Crane, R. (2000). The influence of marital and family therapy on health care utilization in a health maintenance organization. *Journal of Marital and Family Therapy, 26,* 281–292.

Leff, J., Vearnals, S., Brewin, C. R., Wolff, G., Alexander, B., Asen, E., Dayson, D., Jones, E., Chisholm, D., & Everitt, B. (2000). The London depression intervention trial. Randomised controlled trial of anti-depressants vs couple therapy in the treatment and maintenance of people with depression living with a partner: clinical outcome and costs. *British Journal of Psychiatry, 174,* 95–100.

Markus, E., Lange, A., & Pettigrew, T. (1990). Effectiveness of family therapy: a meta-analysis. *Journal of Family Therapy, 12,* 205–221.

Nugent, W., Carpenter, D., & Parks, J. (1993). A statewide evaluation of family preservation and family reunification services. *Research on Social Work Practice, 3,* 40–65.

Pinsof, W., & Wynne, L. (1995). The efficacy of marital and family therapy: an empirical overview, conclusions and recommendations. *Journal of Marital and Family Therapy, 21,* 585–613.

Roth, A., & Fonagy, P. (1996). *What Works For Whom? A critical review of psychotherapy research.* New York: Guilford Press.

Shadish, W., Ragsdale, K., Glaser, R., & Montgomery, L. (1995). The efficacy and effectiveness of marital and family therapy: a perspective from meta-analysis. *Journal of Marital and Family Therapy, 21,* 345–360.

CHAPTER SEVEN

Evidence-based practice and the psychodynamic psychotherapies

P. H. Richardson

What is evidence-based practice?

E vidence-based medicine (EBM) has been defined as: 'the conscientious, explicit and judicious use of current best evidence in making decisions about the care of individual patients. The practice of evidence-based medicine means integrating individual, clinical expertise with the best available external clinical evidence from systematic research' (Sackett D L et al 1996). Evidence-based practice is a broadening, to health care in general, of the principles of EBM.

Fundamental to the evidence-based approach to health care is the idea that equitable provision be guided by standards of evidence concerning the effectiveness of treatments. The gold standard of such evidence has widely been viewed as the randomised controlled trial (RCT) which has now become the dominant method for evaluating drugs and many other treatment methods. The collation of information about the findings of such trials has become a growth industry in recent years and various sources of abstracted information are now available, including the Cochrane library (Cochrane Collaboration, 1999).

An evidence-based approach to health care stands in contra-distinction to conventional methods of medicine in which clinical experience would typically be combined with a knowledge of biological principles to yield a best practice decision in any particular case. Within this perspective, value is given to the notion of clinical authority or expertise and, if a senior colleague cannot provide an immediate source of such expertise, reference can be made to a respected textbook.

Evidence-based practice (EBP) does not eschew the role of clinical experience but simply argues that it is such experience which will complement and enable the appropriate interpretation of available evidence—so that it is only in the absence of an evidence-based approach that reliance upon clinical experience alone becomes inadvisable. The present chapter examines some of the problems which arise when considering an EBP approach in the psychodynamic psychotherapies.

Standards of evidence

A requirement of EBP is that clinical decision making be largely informed by good evidence concerning best practice. What constitutes good evidence might at first be thought to be simple, viz that it is evidence from research carried out with sufficient scientific rigour to be both believable (eg internally valid) and applicable (ie generalisable—or, roughly speaking, externally valid). On this basis, a series of assumptions is made about what constitutes acceptable evidence and a hierarchy of value is typically ascribed to different sources of evidence: RCTs are thought to yield stronger evidence than open case series, which yield stronger evidence than clinician consensus, which may yield stronger evidence than patient views about effectiveness, etc (Dept of Health, 1996a).

Using such a hierarchy it becomes possible to identify the evidential criteria whereby treatments may justifiably be described as empirically 'validated' or 'supported' (NB the latter term is increasingly preferred since it avoids the implication of finality contained within an all-or-none notion of validation. As evidence accumulates treatments can be seen as increasingly supported from an empirical standpoint—Chambless and Hollon, 1998). Lists can then be drawn up of treatments with a sufficiently solid empirical base for use in routine care (and thus, in the USA, for support by public or private health care insurance schemes) and incorporation in clinical guidelines (RCP, 1994)—with the assumption that empirically poorly supported therapies must remain "experimental" until they accumulate adequate empirical support (APA Taskforce, 1995).

Evidence for the benefits of the Psychodynamic Psychotherapies (PDP)

Psychodynamic psychotherapies (PDP) are, for the most part, poorly empirically supported—according to the evidential criteria commonly applied in contemporary reviews (Chambless and Hollon, 1998; Dobson and Craig 1998; Nathan and Gorman 1998; Roth and Fonagy, 1996) For example, in one of the most comprehensive and accomplished comparative psychotherapy outcome reviews, Roth and Fonagy (1996) found that PDP achieved their minimal criteria for full empirical validation only in the treatment of depression for the elderly; and failed to do so for the treatment of any child or adult disorder. Moreover their standards of 'partial validation' were also only achieved by PDP in a handful of conditions. These findings have been largely echoed in several more recent reviews and overviews (DeRubeis and Crits-Cristoph 1998; Dobson and Craig 1998; Nathan and Gorman 1998; Fonagy et al 1999).

On the surface then it would appear that for psychodynamic psychotherapy to be practised within an evidence-based framework an important initial task may be that of gathering the relevant evidence concerning its effects. Much will depend, however, on the ways in which evidence is defined, the kinds of evidence which are acceptable within the framework of evidence based practice, and the special problems which may arise when a set of methodological criteria—developed for the evaluation of research evidence outside the domain of psychotherapy—are applied within that domain. This chapter is largely devoted to exploring these issues.

Which evidential criteria in psychotherapy outcome research

From the Sackett et al definition (above) it might be thought that the primary task of the evidence-based approach is that of identifying good quality evidence. In reality a prior task may be that of determining what constitutes good quality evidence. The standards of scientific acceptability which apply to evidence in the domain of physical medicine may be relatively clear—and subject to relatively common agreement. Those which might properly apply in the domain of psychotherapy (and especially psychodynamic psychotherapy) are less clear and are certainly far from universally agreed (Elliott 1998). Whilst there may be certain core principles which apply widely to the evaluation of treatment methods it also seems probable that each field of enquiry will have—to some extent—its own unique evidential standards.

Examples of the way in which differing standards of evaluation may need to apply in different research domains are numerous. For example, at some stage in the evaluation of any new form of pharmacotherapy it would be expected that the treatment be compared with a placebo. This enables its specific pharmacological impact to be identified when its psychological impact has been controlled for (Pocock 1984). The use of the placebo control condition in psychotherapy research, however, where *all* treatments have a primarily psychological impact, is now regarded as an inappropriate and blunt way in which to identify the specificity of a treatment's effects (Parloff 1986). Various forms of process research may enable the identification of the psychological processes whereby a treatment of demonstrated efficacy has its action (Garfield, 1990), but the placebo control condition has largely been abandoned for this purpose.

Similarly the importance of double-blind methodology in assessing the effects of treatment is axiomatic where pharmacotherapy research is concerned (Pocock, 1984). It is hopelessly impractical—and hence irrelevant—for psychotherapy outcome evaluation. The rationale for using double blind methodology is to minimise the potential biasing effects on patient and/or therapist which may arise from knowledge about and attitudes towards the treatment concerned. Neither patient nor therapist can remain blind to the fact of receiving or giving psychotherapy, however, and once again, more sophisticated methods are needed to examine the extent to which the patient and therapist's knowledge and attitudes influence therapeutic outcome.

In contrast there may be methodological criteria of special relevance to psychotherapy research—which may be of lesser importance in other kinds of treatment trial. An example might be the extent to which the quality of the therapy, which was delivered in the trial, has been demonstrated or can reasonably be assumed. Variations in pill content and quality are likely to be small in drug trials. Variations in the content and quality of psychotherapy could be considerable. Comparative psychotherapy studies involving psychodynamic approaches have sometimes used expert therapists —an example being the Sloan et al (1975) RCT which found psychoanalytic therapy to be equivalent in effectiveness to behaviour therapy and superior to a waiting list control condition. Others have used non-expert therapists—as in the Bellack et al (1980) study—where the psychodynamic therapy was used as a control for non-specific factors and, not surprisingly, was less effective than social skills training or drug treatment.

The list of criteria for assessing methodological quality in outcome studies in any therapy domain is likely to be long. It will include considerations of adequacy of design, sample, measurement, therapy integrity, follow-up periods, data analysis and reporting as well as other features. Scoring criteria have frequently been employed to assess methodological adequacy, particularly for use in systematic reviews (eg Jadad 1998, Shapiro et al 1994), and there is some evidence to suggest that as methodological adequacy drops, so the apparent effects of treatment (ie effect sizes) go up (eg Shapiro et al 1994). At the very least this underlines the importance of paying adequate regard to the evaluative methods employed in individual studies.

In view of the inevitably imperfect nature of applied research, reviewers cannot realistically exclude all studies which fail on a single criterion of methodological adequacy. Thus the relative weighting given to different methodological criteria will influence the likelihood that studies appear in reviews and hence contribute, either positively or negatively, to the evidence base relating to particular therapies. The Bellack et al study, using psychodynamic psychotherapy as a placebo, meets many of the criteria of a good quality study and therefore finds it way into reviews of the efficacy of PDP, albeit as a study that is acknowledged to add little to our understanding of its outcome (Roth & Fonagy 1996). The Sloan study, whilst in some ways providing a far more valid test of (expert) therapy on a (clinically representative) group of mixed neurotic patients, is excluded from some recent reviews for failing to meet the criterion of specificity of patient sample (see below).

The above example reinforces the point that a single set of 'evidence-based' research criteria cannot respond across the board to the needs of reviewers—or of individual clinicians who, in the absence of clear guidelines, are trying to find their way through the maze of research relevant to their particular area of practice. It is a commonplace in scientific circles that two narrative reviews of the same source material may arrive at different conclusions. Clarity is achieved in systematic reviews and meta-analyses through explicit stipulation of the rules whereby individual studies contribute to conclusions. This clarity should not be confused with certainty about the correctness of the chosen rules.

It is not suggested here that, were a differently organised set of cogent scientific criteria applied to the evaluation of outcome studies on PDP, the present dearth of acceptable evidence would suddenly be transformed into a plethora. It is simply proposed that proper attention be paid to the adoption of psychotherapeutically relevant methods in psychotherapy evaluation research.

The RCT as gold standard

It is not difficult to see why the RCT has been largely adopted as the premier paradigm for treatment evaluation research. Findings from individual case studies, however systematically conducted and however compelling, cannot with confidence be applied to larger populations, and single case study methods typically pose problems for the clear identification of a cause-effect relationship between treatment and outcome (Roth and Fonagy 1996). Studies based on groups of patients, selected according to clear criteria, may be more convincing where generalisability is concerned. The use of pre and post treatment measures may enable documentation of change across such patient groups. When controlled (eg by comparing treated patients with others who receive a different or delayed intervention), one may also have greater confidence that the study is not simply tapping the effects of spontaneous symptom fluctuation over time, or an effect of repeated measurement—independently of treatment received.

Without random allocation to the conditions being compared, however, a causal relationship between treatment and outcome cannot be confidently assumed. The two or more groups being compared in a nonrandomised trial may always have been different with respect to some (possibly unidentified) variable, and in such a way that their eventual outcomes following treatment appear spuriously to reflect a true treatment effect, but would in any case always have been different. Randomisation to treatment condition —from the same initial sample—eliminates systematic sources of sample bias and, when combined with explicit matching of groups on key variables (as for example in the minimisation technique— Miller et al, 1980), also reduces the likelihood of chance differences in factors which might confound the valid comparison of outcome across groups. In sum, the inherently experimental design of the RCT affords greater confidence than other designs in the inferred causal relationship between the independent variable (treatment) and the dependent variable (outcome).

Problems with RCTs

There are many problems however with randomised trials as well as with other aspects of the methodology which commonly accompanies the RCT. These have been well summarised elsewhere (eg Jadad, 1998) and will only be selectively sampled here.

Several of the drawbacks of the randomised trial derive from the fact that randomisation as a basis for treatment allocation is highly atypical of the way in which treatments are ordinarily administered in normal clinical practice. This has two implications. Firstly patients who consent to randomisation (or whose therapists consent to their randomisation) may not be typical of patients in general. Secondly the fact of receiving a treatment on the basis of the haphazard choice implied by randomisation may itself influence the psychological impact of the treatment. This may be relatively unimportant where the aim of a trial is to assess the physical impact of a physical treatment but could be critical where psychological treatments are concerned. These factors combine to raise questions about the generalisability of the findings of RCTs to the patient population in general.

It is important to note, however, that a number of the difficulties with RCTs have been addressed elsewhere in treatment evaluation research, and with solutions that may equally apply in the psychotherapy research field. For example the use of an 'intention to treat' design overcomes some of the problems arising from potentially biassed samples (Jadad 1998) and 'patient preference' designs can examine the impact of randomisation per se (Brewin and Bradley 1989) An example of the latter in psychological treatments research is the comparison of randomised with nonrandomised patients treated with CBT in Williams, Nicholas, Richardson et al, (1999). In this study no differences were found in outcome between the two groups, challenging the notion that the use of randomisation inevitably poses a threat to external validity. Nevertheless the external validity of RCTs cannot be automatically assumed and should arguably be tested in effectiveness studies (see below).

Moreover for a randomised controlled trial to give meaningful results about the efficacy of a particular form of therapy it is increasingly recognised that it is necessary to describe clearly the patient group on whom the treatment was tested in the RCT. This leads to the requirement of a relatively homogeneous patient sample and the necessity to exclude cases in which significant comorbidity or other confounding variables may be present. For example if a treatment for depression were shown to be efficacious on a sample of patients who were not only depressed but who, at the same time, suffered from other mental health problems, it might be difficult to know whether the treatment had its effects through a beneficial impact on depression per se or on some other aspect of psychopathology. This may further limit the external validity of studies of this kind in so far as patients without comorbidity may also be atypical of those commonly referred to mental health services.

Efficacy vs Effectiveness

These and similar considerations relating to the methodology of formal treatment trials have given rise to the distinction between the concepts of efficacy and effectiveness. Efficacy studies are the formal controlled treatment trials which ask whether a clearly stipulated treatment approach has particular effects on a precisely defined patient population. Effectiveness research is concerned with whether the treatments in question are actually effective in the context of everyday clinical practice with everyday patients and therapists.

Several reviewers have drawn attention to the potentially limited generalisability of the findings from efficacy studies and of the need for effectiveness studies to be carried out before an evidence based approach can be truly applied.

In addition to the atypical and potentially biassing effects of randomisation and the potentially distorted nature of clinical samples, there are other factors which may enhance the internal and construct validity of efficacy studies, yet reduce the generalisability of their findings. Examples include: (i) the extensive and multifaceted approach to outcome assessment and extensive therapy monitoring which are atypical of clinical practice, (ii) the fact that treatment methods themselves may be atypical—either through an unnatural but enforced standardisation; or the fact that formal trials typically test therapies over shorter treatment periods than apply in routine practice; or because standards of therapeutic practice may be higher in formal trials; and so on. When added to the fact that efficacy studies very often fail to incorporate a long-term follow-up, one can see why a sceptical eye is warranted when considering their clinical relevance. A growing research literature is now addressing the question of clinical representativeness in outcome studies. For a thorough discussion of many of these issues see, for example, Goldfried and Wolfe (1998), Roth and Fonagy (1996) and Shadish et al (1997).

The balance of disadvantage for PDP

The distinction between efficacy and effectiveness research is important when considering the evidence base for the psychotherapies. It is well known for example that the cognitive-behavioural therapies have a far more solid grounding in efficacy research than is currently the case for the psychodynamic psychotherapies (Dept of Health 1996b). The evidence base provided by such efficacy research may be of direct relevance to only a small proportion of the patients who typically access services, however, viz. closely scrutinised and expertly treated patients, who are homogeneously and non-comorbidly depressed—with no associated anxiety or personality disorder, for example—who have agreed to accept treatment by random allocation, etc. With this in mind, the apparent imbalance in the evidence base between cognitive-behavioural and psychodynamic therapies starts to look rather different. This is especially so given that the more 'complex' patients commonly excluded from formal efficacy trials may be the harder ones to help, whose outcomes from the kind of brief therapies for which the evidence base is strongest might be altogether less positive. Moreover the relative dearth of longer term follow-up data from most efficacy studies carried out to date reduces still further their value as an exclusive basis for evidence-based practice. Very little clinical effectiveness research has been carried out on any of the psychological treatments—where most therapeutic models are therefore in a similar position as far as empirical support is concerned (Dept of Health 1996b).

It is worth noting perhaps that the efficacy/effectiveness distinction can be overstated (cf Chambless and Hollon, 1998): although the requirements for establishing different forms of validity (eg internal vs external) are very often in conflict they are not *necessarily* so. RCT methodology is not the exclusive preserve of efficacy studies. For all its problems, it is equally applicable and equally relevant to effectiveness research (cf pragmatic trials). Likewise efficacy studies can be designed wherever possible with clinical representativeness in mind (Shadish et al 1997).

Special problems of efficacy research in PDP

It is clear therefore that evidence-based practice is far from straightforward. The difficulties in interpreting evidence in general (eg the problems of interpreting efficacy studies), and the distinctive characteristics of psychotherapy research itself (eg the problem of weighting quality of therapy in the hierarchy of value ascribed to methodological criteria) combine to suggest that the relevant evidence-base for psychotherapy practice will not always be evident. In addition there are a number of problems which become particularly acute when seeking to apply an evidence-based approach to the psychodynamic psychotherapies.

Categorising the Relevant Evidence

For evidence about treatment effectiveness to be usable by individual clinicians it needs to be collated according to classificatory principles which make it accessible. Predetermined categories of evidence can then be applied to predetermined categories of patient problem/characteristic, identified by diagnostic criteria or some other system of classification. If patient x presents with disorder y for which the treatment of choice is p—(ie p has been shown to be the most efficacious in a randomised controlled trial), then an evidence-based approach to patient care would support the choice of treatment p.

In keeping with the medical roots of much psychotherapy, and perhaps for lack of a better classificatory principle, reviews of evidence typically organise findings around diagnostically identified patient groups. The reasoning behind this is simple. Without being clear to which group a particular set of findings might apply, it is impossible to know how to interpret or apply those findings (Roth and Fonagy, 1996). Findings on the outcome of psychotherapy for patients with depression may have a different meaning from those on psychotherapy for anxiety. This will be especially so when it is known that the ordinary clinical course of different disorders, without treatment, will vary. Insofar as treatment response can be relativised to a particular patient group, the generalisability of the associated findings is easier to assess. (NB The otherwise excellent RCT by Sloan et al (1975)—mentioned above—looked at mixed neurotic patients and therefore, as a test of the efficacy of PDP, is limited in what it can tell us, owing to its lack of specificity with regard to the treated conditions).

A fear commonly expressed among psychotherapists is that in its simplest form this approach to evidence-based practice might seem to imply that the complexity of the individual case could be reduced to a single unitary theme or classificatory principle. Thus in depression, say, the assumption would be that what it is that depressives have most in common with each other (ie the characteristic features of depression) will be more relevant to treatment choice and outcome than all those features and characteristics that are individual, and thus vary across patients.

A simple approach in which identification of a particular disorder implies choice of a particular treatment presumably works well for those conditions (eg infectious diseases) where individual differences may moderate treatment *response*, but will not strongly affect treatment *choice*. It may also dovetail better with an approach to psychological treatment that focusses primarily on overt symptoms or problems, eg behaviour therapy.

If, on the other hand, individual differences in factors other than illness/problem category were highly predictive of outcome then such an approach might encounter difficulties. Suppose, for example, it were shown that patient preference for particular treatment styles (eg for prescriptive as opposed to exploratory therapist behaviour), or some other individual difference variable, were related to psychological treatment outcome in depression, say. This would reduce the applicability of a simple model where diagnosis-x-implies-treatment-y. (NB the relevance of aptitude-treatment interaction (ATI) studies to psychotherapy outcome research is increasingly being explored—cf Shoham and Rohrbaugh 1995).

This complicating factor is not problematic for a simple model of evidence based practice to the extent that the additional evidence (in this case about patient preference) can be built into the algorithm which would tell us, here, that depressed patients with preference 'a' might be treated with treatment 'x', while those with preference 'b' could be treated with approach 'y'. This works fine and can fit comfortably within a formal diagnostic perspective *for as long as the superordinate classificatory principle remains that of the disorder being treated*, in this case depression. If treatment preference, or some other individual difference variable, were found to be more strongly predictive of outcome than problem category then the problem of organising and consequently accessing the relevant evidence—to enable an evidence based approach—becomes more complex. It is no longer a disorder that is being treated but a person.

Process and outcome research to date suggest that neither treatment modality nor psychiatric diagnostic status account for more than a very limited proportion of outcome variance (cf Garfield 1998). As with other psychological treatments, research on PDP must attempt to identify those individual difference dimensions of greatest relevance to predicting outcome if an evidence-based approach to psychotherapy is to become more than a pale imitation of a medical formulary.

Problems with the use of psychiatric diagnosis

ICD and DSM diagnoses are bio-behavioural in nature and in that sense might be considered to be more facilitatory in the evaluation of outcome research findings for biological or behavioural/cognitive treatments. Psychodynamic approaches to psychotherapy generally use a different set of diagnostic criteria, with the result that a generalised set of claims concerning the effectiveness of that treatment cannot be made specifically in relation to formal diagnoses. The theoretical basis underlying psychodynamic approaches to psychotherapy would not lead to the conclusion that they will be effective in every case of depression, say. Indeed from a psychodynamic standpoint the lack of specificity of psychiatric diagnostic categories renders them largely uninformative. A diagnosis of anxiety may be no more meaningful to a psychodynamic psychotherapist than a diagnosis of chest pain to a respiratory physician or stomach pain to a gastroenterologist. These would not be regarded as diagnostic categories, so much as symptoms of any number of possible underlying disorders. This might imply that an alternative set of classificatory principles would be expected to be more predictive of the outcome of psychodynamic psychotherapy. Whether this is so or not remains, for the time being, an unanswered empirical question. Future studies could usefully address the relative predictive power of formal diagnoses and psychodynamic formulations in the prediction of psychodynamic psychotherapy outcome.

This leads us on to a further consideration that is specific to the evaluation of psychodynamic psychotherapies, viz. the significance of the dynamic unconscious. As has been noted elsewhere (eg Roth and Fonagy 1996), formal ICD and DSM diagnoses take no account of unconscious processes in evaluating patients and cannot therefore be seen as highly consistent with an approach to treatment based heavily upon such factors. Similarly excluded by formal diagnostic categories is the developmental perspective. Formal psychiatric diagnoses say little or nothing about aetiology and yet from a psychodynamic standpoint, aetiological considerations may have great importance for choice of treatment approach. For example, in cases of childhood sexual abuse, resultant mental health problems could later take the form of anxiety, depression or some other psychopathology. To speak of the treatment of anxiety or the treatment of depression in such cases would be meaningless, when in fact the therapeutic work would be affected predominantly by considerations of the sexual abuse itself.

For these reasons, an evidence-based approach built around the collation of evidence, which is structured by formal diagnoses, may be of limited relevance to the evaluation of treatment trials related to psychodynamic psychotherapy.

Limitations of the Drug Metaphor

If the use of formal diagnoses, as a framework for collating evidence about psychotherapy outcomes, highlights difficulties with a simplistic illness model for psychological problems, then consideration of the nature of psychotherapy itself may underline the limitations of the 'drug metaphor' (Stiles and Shapiro 1989). EBM implies application of a treatment to a disorder. In the same way that the disorder is satisfactorily summarised by a particular diagnostic description, so the treatment is seen as a distinctive entity to be 'applied', almost as one might apply a poultice or an antibiotic. This ignores the evolutionary and potentially self-correcting nature of therapy and, within that, the central role of the therapeutic relationship in creating (ie not just mediating) the therapeutic process. Stiles and Shapiro (1989) provide numerous examples of the limitations of conventional process-outcome research founded on the principle that identifiable treatment ingredients will have a simple and unidirectional impact on treatment outcome. Moreover Shapiro et al (1994) have demonstrated the very limited mileage to be obtained from process-outcome research based on such premises. These considerations are likely to be especially problematic in the therapies, like PDP, for which the therapeutic relationship is viewed as central, rather than simply facilitative—as in CBT.

Evaluation of long term therapies

Special problems arise in the accumulation of an evidence base concerning long-term therapies—some relating to study design, others to cost-effectiveness. Examples will be given of each.

Where design is concerned, it is a requirement of a randomised trial to have a comparison condition assessed at the same end points on relevant outcome measures as the treated group (Jadad 1998). The comparison condition typically involves either minimal or no treatment on the one hand or a treatment of known effectiveness on the other hand. Comparison of long term psychodynamic psychotherapy with no treatment poses particular design problems if the psychodynamic psychotherapy is likely to be so long term that it is unrealistic (and unethical) to expect a no treatment control group to go without treatment for the entire period of the trial. Yet unless treated and untreated patients can be compared at equivalent endpoints this contaminates the comparison between therapy and its absence.

This problem can sometimes be overcome by the use of a minimal treatment control condition which may or may not be given to both groups of patients ie. those who also receive the treatment being evaluated and those who do not. In this case the evaluation of the formal treatment takes the form of assessing its incremental benefits relative to the minimal treatment.

In areas where brief treatments may have only very limited effectiveness it may be argued that more efficacious longer term treatment may also be more cost-effective. Where cost-effectiveness is concerned, however, Maynard (1997)has pointed out that factors affecting treatment choice within an evidence-based framework may be quite different when seen from the perspective of population health (eg by commissioners of services) than those which might be applied on an individual basis by a clinician considering the needs of his/her individual patient.

Take for example a conventional treatment costing £1,000 and extending survival time in a terminal disease by one year. A new treatment costing £4,000 might be found to increase life expectancy by two years. The clinician, adopting an evidence-based approach, will choose treatment B over treatment A since it offers the best prospect for the individual patient. Health economists however would recommend the use of treatment A because, for a given sum of money, a greater number of life years can be purchased for the population as a whole. In this case, for £8,000, eight life years can be purchased by the conventional treatment where only four life years can be purchased by the newer treatment. Thus, where health care resources will always be limited, economic considerations will always temper the extent to which longer term therapies may be recommended—a consideration of potential importance to the psychodynamic therapies.

There are few who would question the fundamental laudability of evidence-based practice as a guiding principle in medicine and as a healthy corrective to maverick individualism. At the same time we have seen enough in the present chapter to appreciate that the adoption of an evidence-based approach in psychotherapy may generate significant problems of both conceptual and practical varieties. Conceptual problems include the facts that neither people nor treatments can be described simply. Practical ones include the dilemma that while the RCT may be the only convincing method currently available to investigate causality in the relation between treatment and outcome, nevertheless the recognition of this fact should not lead us to forget that it is also, in many ways, lamentably inadequate to the task.

In its selective overview, the present chapter has failed to address numerous aspects of outcome research methodology which may have significance for the evaluation of pychodynamic psychotherapy. These include problems associated with appropriate choice of outcome measures and, in particular, the use of dynamic criteria in assessing patient progress; the benefits and demerits of single case and other (eg qualitative) research methodologies in evaluating PDP; problems associated with standardisation, and in particular manualisation, of therapeutic methods; measurement reactivity problems which may arise when investigating therapy adherence and other approaches to assessing treatment integrity.

Ard then of course we should not forget that, in psychoanalytic circles, there is a substantial body of opinion which would question the fundamental epistemology underlying modern empirical approaches to the evaluation of therapeutic activity (eg Perron, 1999).

There are indications, however, that psychodynamic psychotherapy researchers are rising at last to the challenges posed by formal outcome research. In a recent hotly contested initiative to promote psychoanalytic research, the International Psychoanalytical Association received more applications to fund outcome research than for any other category of investigation (Wallerstein and Fonagy 1999). Moreover a recently published open-door review of outcome studies in psychoanalysis and psychoanalytic psychotherapy testifies to the wealth of high quality ongoing studies in this domain (Fonagy et al 1999). These should bearing fruit in the coming decade. Better late than never!

References

APA Task Force (1995) *Template for Developing Guidelines: Interventions for Mental Disorders and Psychological Aspects of Physical Disorders.* Washington, DC: American Psychological Association.

Bellack A S, Hersen M and Himmelhoch J M (1981) Social Skills Training Compared with Pharmacotherapy and Psychotherapy for Depression. *American Journal of Psychiatry,* **138,** pp. 1562–1567.

Brewin C R and Bradley C (1989) Patient Preferences and Randomised Clinical Trials. *British Medical Journal,* **299,** pp. 313–315.

Chambless D L and Hollon S D (1998) Defining Empirically Supported Therapies *Journal of Consulting and Clinical Psychology* **66,** pp. 7–18.

Cochrane Collaboration (1999) *The Cochrane Library.* Oxford: Update Software, [available via the Internet or on CD-ROM].

DeRubeis RJ and Crits-Cristoph P (1998) Empirically supported group and individual treatments for adult psychological disorders. *Therapies Journal of Consulting and Clinical Psychology* **66,** pp. 37–52

Dept of Health (1996a) *Promoting Clinical Effectiveness: A framework for action in and through the NHS.* London: NHS Executive

Dept of Health (1996b) *Psychotherapy Services in England: Review of Strategic Policy.* London: NHS Executive

Dobson KS and Craig KD (Eds) (1998) *Empirically Supported Therapies: Best Practice in Professional Psychology*. Thousand Oaks: Sage Publications

Elliott R (1998) A Guide to the Empirically Supported Treatments Controversy, *Psychotherapy Research*, **8**, 115–125

Fonagy P, Kaechele H, Krause R, Jones E, Perron R (1999) *An Open Door Review of Outcome Studies in Psychoanalysis* London: UCL Psychoanalysis Unit. (and available at http://www.ipa.org.uk/R-outcome.htm)

Garfield S (1990) Issues and Methods in psychotherapy process research. *Journal of Consulting and Clinical Psychology*, **58(3)** 273–280

Garfield S (1998) Some Comments on Empirically Supported Treatments, *Journal of Consulting and Clinical Psychology*, **66**, pp. 121–125

Goldfried MR and Wolfe BE (1998) towards a more clinically valid approach to therapy research. *Journal of Consulting and Clinical Psychology*, **66**, 143–150

Kendall PC, (1998) Empirically Supported Psychological Therapies, *Journal of Consulting and Clinical Psychology*, **66**, pp. 3–6.

Jadad A (1998) *Randomised Controlled Trials*, London: BMJ Books

Maynard A (1997) Evidence-based medicine: an incomplete method for informing treatment choices. *Lancet* **349(9045):** 126–128

Miller RG, Efron B, Brown BW, et al (1980) *BioStatistics Casebook*, New York: Wiley.

Nathan PE and Gorman JM (1998) *A Guide to Treatments that Work*. New York: Oxford University Press

Parloff MB (1986) Placebo controls in psychotherapy research: A sine qua non or a placebo for research problems? Special Issue: Psychotherapy research. *Journal of Consulting and Clinical Psychology*; **54(1)** 79–87

Perron R (1999) Reflections on Psychoanalytic Research Problems—the French-Speaking View. In P Fonagy et al: *An Open Door Review of Outcome Studies in Psychoanalysis*. London: UCL Psychoanalysis Unit

Pocock S J (1984) *Clinical Trials: A Practical Approach*, Chichester: Wiley.

RCP (1994) *Clinical Practice Guidelines and Their Development*. Council Report CR34, Royal College of Psychiatrists, London

Roth A and Fonagy P (1996) *What works for whom? A critical review of psychotherapy research* New York: Guilford

Sackett D L et al (1996). *Evidence-based Medicine: What is it and What it isn't*. BMJ 312 (7023) 13th January, 71–72.

Shadish WR, Matt GE, Navarro AM, Siegle g et al (1997) Evidence that treatment works in clinically representative conditions. *Journal of Consulting and Clinical Psychology* **65(3),** 355–365

Shapiro DA, Harper H, Startup M, Reynolds S, Bird D, Suokas A (1994) The High Water Mark of the Drug Metaphor: A Meta-analytic Critique of Process-Outcome Research. In Russell RL (Ed) *Reassessing Psychotherapy Research* New York: Guilford, pp 1–35

Shoham V and Rohrbaugh M (1995) Aptitude x Treatment Interaction (ATI) Research. In: M Aveline and D A Shapiro *Research Foundations for Psychotherapy Practice*, Chichester: Wyley pp. 73–96.

Sloan R B, Staples F R, cristol A H, Yorkston N J and Whipple K (1975) *Psychotherapy Versus Behaviour Therapy*, Cambridge, M A: Harvard University Press.

Stiles W B and Shapiro D A (1989) Abuse of the Drug Metaphor in Psychotherapy Process-Outcome Research. *Clinical Psychology Review*, 9, pp. 521–543.

Williams, A.CdeC., Nicholas, M.K., Richardson, P.H., et al (1999). Generalizing from a controlled trial: the effects of patient preference versus randomization on the outcome of inpatient versus outpatient chronic pain management. *Pain*, 83. 57–65.

Wallerstein R and Fonagy P (1999) Psychoanalytic research and the IPA: history, present status and future potential. *International Journal of Psychoanalysis*, **80,** 91–109

PART II:
CLINICAL AUDIT

CHAPTER EIGHT

Audit cycle

T he term "audit" is usually associated with finance and accounting. Clinical audit is a different process. It is a process of **systematically reviewing and improving the quality of care we give to patients**. It is a continuous process rather than a finite project and is best conceptualized as a cycle. The following Chapters give guidance on each stage of the audit cycle, as illustrated in *Figure 3* on p. 72.

1. Choose a topic

Why clinical audit?

There may be different reasons for selecting a particular area to audit. Some of these are outlined below:

- To improve your own or your team's functioning: you may notice, through experience or anecdotes of your colleagues, that for example you are getting more/less DNAs, more/less referrals from primary care etc. In any such case you could use audit to try and find out if there has been a change, reasons

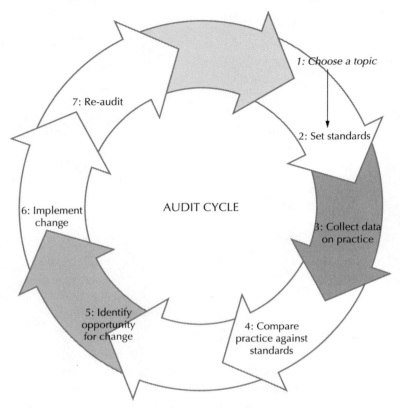

Figure 3. The audit cycle.

for the change, and if you need to adapt or make changes to your service correspondingly.

- Demonstrating the usefulness of your service: you may feel that your service is under threat owing to, for example, beliefs that it is not useful or effective. Audit can be used to defend the service from internal or external threats of this nature. An audit of self-referrals by the Adolescent Department of the Tavistock Clinic in London was used in this way to counter the opinion that patients tended to be not severely mentally ill but merely the "worried well" (Upson & Wright, 1999).

- Campaigning for resources: you may find that you are providing a service that is not recognized as using the quantity of resources you actually use and is thus insufficiently funded. An audit can be used to demonstrate the funding required for the service and can be used as a bargaining tool to acquire this.

- External requirements: there are some instances in which a Health Authority or the NHS-Executive will require that a particular audit be carried out. For example your service agreement with a Health Authority may include the requirement for you to meet certain standards regarding communication with referrers. The 1998 White paper also states that the National Institute for Clinical Excellence (established April 1999) will have the authority to place requirements on Trusts to participate in any appropriate National Confidential Enquiries. You may therefore have to participate in the National Confidential Inquiry into Homicide and Suicide.
- Service User involvement: refer to "Involving Health Service Users" in Chapter Fifteen. This addresses ways in which service users may be involved in clinical audit. Service users may be involved at any stage of clinical audit, providing they are provided with sufficient training or support. However, a particularly important stage at which to involve users is in the selection of topics which are of concern to them.

Service areas and quality domains

Donabedian (1966) divided quality investigations into the following three service areas:

- Structure: this refers to structural aspects of the organization, for example suitability of waiting rooms, appointment systems, equipment, staffing levels, usability, and contents of patient notes etc.
- Process: this refers to the procedural aspects of the service, for example the appropriateness of assessments and treatments, communication between professionals and patients or their relatives, continuity of care etc.
- Outcome: this refers to the effectiveness and efficiency of the treatments, such as clinical outcomes, cost-effectiveness, quality of life, and patient satisfaction.

Firth-Cozens (1993) divides quality domains into eight areas:

- Equity;
- Access;
- Acceptability and responsiveness;
- Appropriateness;
- Communication;
- Continuity;
- Effectiveness; and
- Efficiency.

Service areas and quality domains can be thought of as a matrix—although there is significant overlap between cells in the matrix. Examples of audits that may fit into each cell are given in *Table 1*. The matrix is adapted from Firth-Cozens (1993).

Table 1. Examples of topics for audit (Adapted from Firth-Cozens, 1993, p. 25).

	Structure	*Process*	*Outcome*
Equity and access	Disabled access. Interpreters. Expenses for travel. Flexibility of appointment times.	Waiting times for assessment. Pathways to care of ethnic minorities. Procedures for illiterate patients. Choice of therapist (according to gender/race/religion).	Does DNA rate reduce when patients are given choice of therapist?
Acceptability and responsiveness	Patient satisfaction with waiting rooms, treatment rooms. Do the services offered reflect patient needs?	Responsiveness to patient needs— frequency of appointments, times of appointments.	Acceptable outcomes in terms of quality of life, family dynamics, work commitments etc.
Appropriateness	Are there appropriately trained staff for the types of patient seen?	Are particular client groups seeing appropriate levels and types of professional? Are assessments appropriate? Are appropriate measures used to assess risk?	Does DNA rate reduce when appropriate assessments conducted? Does treatment outcome improve?

Continued . . .

Table 1. Continued ...

	Structure	Process	Outcome
Communication	Are notes maintained in acceptable manner? Is it easy to access information on patients? Are there adequate confidentiality procedures?	Do GPs receive sufficient information? Is communication between team members acceptable? Is communication to relatives and clients about treatment options clear?	Are outcomes and recommendations communicated to appropriate agencies i.e. GP/ referrer/parents etc.?
Continuity	Are good quality notes maintained to facilitate continuity of care?	Do patients have continuity of care from one professional when possible?	Are appropriate referrals made when patient discharged? Are there appropriate communications to ensure continuity of care?
Effectiveness	Does the PAS supply the information we need?	Is attendance sufficient for effective therapeutic intervention?	Are outcomes in brief interventions as good as they should be? Are outcomes at follow-up as good as they should be?
Efficiency	Are procedures for reducing DNAs being followed? Is best use being made of IT resources that improve efficiency?	Is treatment given only when necessary? Do multiple assessment sessions improve treatment planning?	Is outcome improved by greater therapeutic input?

2. Setting standards

The clinical audit process is directly dependent on clinical standards and guidelines (and/or policies).

The function of a clinical audit project is to:

(1) present evidence that standards are being adhered to; and
(2) find out whether the standards are acceptable or whether they should be modified or enhanced.

Definitions (see examples below)

- Criterion: "the statement of care that is decided in advance that uses words or phrases that make it measurable"
- Standard: "the expression of a range of acceptable variation from a normal criterion".

See Part V for further examples of audit criteria.

Setting standards in the absence of existing standards

LOCAL CONSENSUS

- Determine what common professional practice occurs within your department/unit by carrying out a "baseline" or "service" audit of practice, i.e. you assess in detail what you do and then formulate standards or guidelines based on this.
- Consult users or referrers where appropriate.

NATIONAL CONSENSUS

- Carry out a literature search to see what others are doing in your field and what evidence there is relating to best practice.
- Find out if there are any standards or guidelines already available from Royal Colleges, Patient's Charter, British Psychological Society, local Health Authorities or the National Institute for Clinical Excellence, from which standards can be developed.

EXAMPLE: REFERRER COMMUNICATION STANDARDS.

Criterion   An initial detailed letter must be written to the referrer within two weeks of the end of an assessment

Standard   This criterion must be met in 90% of cases

---

3. Collecting data

Quantitative data

Sources of data may be as follows.

- Routine data: information can be extracted from data that has been collected as part of routine practice, mostly kept in patient files. The most common audits, based on routine data, are audits of quality of casenotes and referrer communication.
- Data collected specifically for audit: data can be collected for the purpose of the audit, for example through a questionnaire or survey, focusing on the questions being looked at in the audit.

It is important that data collection forms, which are used to extract information from routine data, must not be confused with other forms, e.g. questionnaires which are designed to collect specific information.

EXAMPLE: REFERRER COMMUNICATION STANDARDS

Criterion: An initial detailed letter must be written to the referrer within two weeks of the end of an assessment.

1. A data collection form could be used to extract this information from a set of files:
   Date of completion of assessment _____

	Yes	No	N/A
Is there a detailed letter sent to referrer within two weeks of this date			

2. A questionnaire could be sent to the referrer including the questions:

   We completed the assessment of X on _____.
   How long after this date did you receive a detailed letter about the assessment and its outcome?

Number of days	

Qualitative data

- Qualitative approaches are associated with methods of collecting data, such as observation, interviewing, focus groups, open ended questionnaires etc. Using a qualitative technique for audit is very useful when you have very little information to hand on what you are trying to investigate, or you want more in depth information than you can get from a questionnaire, e.g. patients' views on a particular aspect of your service.
- Once you have obtained the information that you want from any particular qualitative technique, this can then be used for making changes to your service or practice, or to develop more quantitative techniques for examining or developing standards for your service.

4. Compare practice against standards

Comparing practice against standards essentially means that the data collected needs to be turned into a form that indicates to what extent the standards set at the beginning of an audit are being met. This requires some form of data analysis. It is important to consider, when planning the audit, how this will be done and by whom. Analysing data for audit is usually much simpler than analysing research data. What is commonly required is no more than simple percentages.

You should be able to say for each criterion for every case in your sample whether it has been met, not met or is not applicable to the case.

EXAMPLE FROM AN AUDIT OF REFERRER COMMUNICATION STANDARDS

On inspecting 60 casenotes, it was found that eight patients never attended for assessment and two were transferred to other services during the assessment, leaving 50. Of these, 37 (37/50 = 74%) had a detailed letter to the referrer following assessment, but only 32 (32/50 = 64%) had been sent within two weeks. This reveals a substantial failure to meet the standard which was set at 90%.

Comparing practice against standards

If you have set a target standard, such as in the case of Referrer Communication in which 90% of cases should meet the criteria, then you can compare your percentage to this and see how much improvement needs to be made.

If you have not set a specific target then you will need to make judgements about whether the percentages are acceptable or not. To do this you could compare them to previous audits of the same criteria or you could compare them to the standards being reached in other services or departments.

5. Identify opportunity for improvement

By the time an audit has reached the stage of data collection and analysis, the responsibility for it has usually devolved to one or two people. It is important, once the results are available, to put the audit back in the hands of the team, unit or department as quickly as possible. The results should be fed back, preferably in a meeting largely or entirely devoted to discussing the audit.

Planning the meeting

The discussion should be largely unstructured so that members of the team have the opportunity to give their own comments and ideas about the results and maintain "ownership" of the audit. However, it is useful to plan how to prevent the discussion from losing a focus and not reaching any conclusions.

- Circulate a brief summary of the audit results in advance of the meeting to give people a chance to consider some thoughts.
- It may be helpful first of all to speak for five minutes about the purpose of the meeting and how it fits into the audit cycle. It may be helpful for your department Audit Lead or the Clinical Audit Facilitator to attend the meeting for this purpose.
- Be aware that most people will not have read the summary circulated before the meeting, so it may be helpful to summarize the results and highlight the important issues.
- Try to pre-empt some of the questions that may be raised, for

example, make sure you are aware of which standards or criteria are externally imposed and which can be negotiated or decided by the team. This will avoid a discussion about whether a particular criterion should be modified when it is in any case non-negotiable.

- Think about how to conclude a meeting particularly if time is short and it is unlikely that all the necessary decisions and conclusions will be reached. For example, you could propose that following the discussion you will draw up a proposal to which clinicians can give individual feedback before final decisions are made.
- Make sure relevant heads of services, professions or of the department are involved in taking things on.

WHERE CAN IMPROVEMENTS BE MADE?

The discussion should focus on where and how changes are to be made. It will be important to emphasize that changes can be made in several different areas—the function of audit is not only to identify problems with clinical practice and find ways of changing it. Some areas where changes could be made are given below:

- review, modify or enhance the standards/criteria themselves;
- changes to clinical practice;
- changes to training or induction procedures; and
- changes to organizational or administrative practice/procedures.

6. Implement change

The most difficult part of undertaking a clinical audit project is in implementing any changes in practice which may be required. Clinical audit is a mechanism through which change management occurs. It is essential that the change processes associated with clinical audit are given as much emphasis as the audit itself, and that change, in terms of new or modified standards, education to improve practice, and any other changes are carried out.

Once the need for change has been identified, the project lead will be responsible for implementing the changes. The following is some initial guidance for managing change.

- Draw up a set of recommendations based on discussions with the team/department and individual feedback. Make sure that the recommendations are agreed by the team.
- Decide what level of authority is required to implement the change. For example, can the team or department make a decision about it or does it need to be agreed by a Department or Discipline Committee or at Board level.
- Decide what resources will be required and what networks of communication will be required to implement the changes.
- Circulate your recommendations to everyone who will take part in or be affected by the changes.
- Inform the Trust Audit Lead or Clinical Audit Department of any changes made and request any support that may be required to enable them to be made. Copy to Chair of Department, Service or Discipline.
- Think about what problems you might face trying to implement changes and pre-empt them.

For further ideas on how to effectively manage change, see Leigh (1988).

7. Re-audit

Re-auditing is an essential part of the audit cycle. Its purpose is to identify what impact the audit has had. Ideally, it will find that standards have been improved following the changes made to practice. It may, however, find that standards have not improved or have even gone down which may indicate that the changes made did not target the source of the problem or that the source of the problem has changed and that the results need to be reconsidered and other angles analysed. It is important to agree a timescale for re-audit when planning the audit and that it is thought of as part of the audit process, not as a separate audit.

Audit cycle or audit spiral?

Because part of the audit process involves making changes to practice, a re-audit can never be identical to the initial audit. As the process continues, with re-audit after re-audit, the criteria, standards and practice being audited should all gradually change. Instead of an audit cycle, the process is therefore more like a spiral in which, it is hoped, improvement is a continuous feature.

EXAMPLE: COMMUNICATION WITH GPS AND REFERRERS

This audit was carried out in the Tavistock Clinic Child and Family department in 1997 lead by Rita Harris (Harris, 1998).

In a recent survey of GPs views of the institution, feedback suggested that staff were often perceived as being poor communicators, in terms of speed, frequency and content of individuals' responses to their referrals. Whether or not this assertion was justified, it required attention. Not only would more effective communication improve patient care, but also GPs will increasingly be the gate-keepers of services.

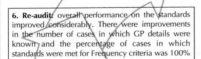

1. Setting standards: these were developed from a literature review, discussions with local GPs, informal and formal discussions with staff within the organisation and with the head of Contracting. Standards were set for the frequency of communications e.g. within two weeks of completion of assessment etc.; and for the format and content. A target of 100% was set for the frequency section and 80% for the format/content section.

6. Re-audit: overall performance on the standards improved considerably. There were improvements in the number of cases in which GP details were known and the percentage of cases in which standards were met for Frequency criteria was 100%

2. Collecting data: data were collected retrospectively from all new cases from 1/4/97–15/5/97. A data collection checklist was devised which had a list of the criteria and met/not met and not applicable columns to tick each case.

5. Implementing change: It was decided that no referrals would be accepted without GP details, even if permission to contact the GP was denied and a template letter was devised to incorporate key information into any correspondence with referrers. The criteria were also reviewed and some changes made where criteria were unreasonable or too vague or poorly worded. These standards were the basis for the current trust standards for referrer communications.

3. Compare practice against standards: the proportion of times that each criterion was met/not met was calculated, presented as percentages and compared with the standards set. A standard was considered not to be applicable to a set of casenotes when the data were not yet available.

4. Identify opportunity for improvement: GP details were found to be absent in a surprising number of cases. Routine information required by GPs was sometimes found to be missing.

EXAMPLE: ACCESS TO SERVICES FOR CLIENTS FROM ETHNIC MINORITIES: ADDRESSING EQUITY IN PSYCHOTHERAPY SERVICES

Equity issues cover a wide range of possible areas for audit. This example focuses mainly on waiting times. It could also be adapted to other equity issues such as disability, gender, social class etc.

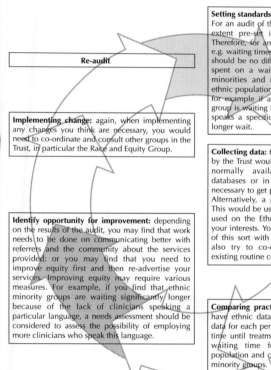

Setting standards
For an audit of this type, the standard is to a large extent pre-set in that equity is the standard. Therefore, for any aspect of service being audited e.g. waiting times, the standard would be that there should be no difference between the average time spent on a waiting list for members of ethnic minorities and members of the white majority ethnic population. There may be exceptions to this, for example if a person from an ethnic minority group is waiting for an interpreter or clinician who speaks a specific language, then there may be a longer wait.

Re-audit

Implementing change: again, when implementing any changes you think are necessary, you would need to co-ordinate and consult other groups in the Trust, in particular the Race and Equity Group.

Collecting data: for this audit, ethnic data collected by the Trust would be required. These data are not normally available from patient electronic databases or in the case file and it would be necessary to get permission to get hold of the data. Alternatively, a prospective audit may be done. This would be useful if you find that the categories used on the Ethnicity Form are not sufficient for your interests. You would need to discuss a project of this sort with the Race and Equity Group and also try to co-ordinate your project with the existing routine collection of data.

Identify opportunity for improvement: depending on the results of the audit, you may find that work needs to be done on communicating better with referrers and the community about the services provided; or you may find that you need to improve equity first and then re-advertise your services. Improving equity may require various measures. For example, if you find that ethnic minority groups are waiting significantly longer because of the lack of clinicians speaking a particular language, a needs assessment should be considered to assess the possibility of employing more clinicians who speak this language.

Comparing practice against standards: once you have ethnic data and corresponding waiting time data for each period e.g. time until assessment and time until treatment, you could calculate a mean waiting time for the white majority ethnic population and compare it with the mean time for minority groups.

References

Donabedian, A. (1966). Evaluating the quality of medical care. *Millbank Memorial Foundation of Quality*, *44*: 166–208.

Firth-Cozens, J. (1993). *Audit in Mental Health Services*. UK: Erlbaum.

Harris, R. (1998). Clinical audit of communication between child mental health professionals and general practitioners. In: E. Hardman & C. Joughin (Eds), *FOCUS on Clinical Audit in Child and Adolescent Mental Health Services*. London: College Research Unit, The Royal College of Psychiatrists.

Leigh, A. (1988). *Effective Change: Twenty ways to make it happen*. London: Institute of Personnel Management.

Upson, P., & Wright, J. (1999). Self-referrals, another outbreak of the "worried well". *Clinical Psychology Forum, 134*: 18–21.

CHAPTER NINE

Audit and research—untangling the ball of string

Mark Charny

W hy bother with the distinction? After all, Shakespeare wrote that a rose by any other name smells as sweet and Humpty Dumpty thought a word meant what he wanted it to mean, the only question was who was master. But it does matter. Some of the reasons for being clear about what audit is and what it isn't are set out below.

Budgets. In primary and secondary care, clinical audit budgets are usually stretched. There is a big R&D budget centrally, and SIFT. Health Authorities have money for public work locally (needs assessment, lifestyle surveys etc.). Trusts have responsibilities to monitor patient satisfaction, Charter standards etc. Money spent on one thing is not available for something else. So being clear about what falls legitimately within or outside a budget is very important for everyone.

Work programmes. Budgets represent available resources. Work programmes represent what has to be achieved with those resources. In a more contractual and performance managed environment, more is expected in terms of deliverables, while room for manoeuvre in the budget is consistently diminishing. Generally, you get no points for achieving something that is not in your objectives. If your objective is for example improving patient care through audit, no amount of published research however good is going to count in your favour when it comes to reviewing your performance.

Responsibility. Most people have a well-developed sense of responsibility. But juggling with competing priorities is difficult at the best of times, and it is helpful to know what should be passed on to someone else and, of course, what you should accept from others.

Methodology. In general, it helps to see clearly what you are trying to achieve so that you can choose the most efficient and effective way of getting there. In research, for example, there are a (small) number of standard ways of conducting a study (RCT, cross-sectional study, cohort study, case-control study etc.). The reason there are a small number is because experience over many years has shown that these approaches have distinct uses and that other methods are not so good. Experience has also taught us the (unique) strengths and weaknesses of each study design. Similarly, methods have developed in audit, though these are not yet as clearly understood as in research—audit hasn't been around so long. Methodology is like choosing the tool for the job. If you don't know what the job is, you can't choose a tool with any sense of confidence.

Ethics. Research must first be approved by a Local Research Ethics Committee. If it isn't, you cannot get it published and you leave yourself open to professional censure and perhaps legal action. Just calling something 'audit' does not make it an audit: it's what the project is that counts. Ethics committees have a large workload and should not be asked to consider audits, but everyone locally should know what research is so that they can pass proposals to the Committee for approval when they should.

Distinguishing audit and research

Research answers the question: what should we do and how should we do it? Audit answers the question: are we doing what we should do in the way we should be doing it?

Research is intended to explore cause and effect relationships:

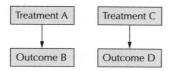

Which treatment gives better outcomes? If we do A, then B tends to happen more often than if we do C. To answer a question like this, we have to isolate A from C from other possible causes which make B more or less likely, so that we can know we are comparing A with C, without the complications of taking into account other factors (D, E, F etc) which may affect the outcome.

On the other hand, the audit cycle is quite different.

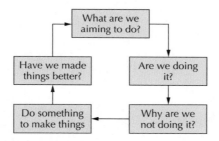

It asks questions about why things are not the way they should be, but the 'why' question is organisational, not scientific. In an audit, the answer to the question 'why are patients getting more bed sores in this hospital than elsewhere?' might be for example:

- we do not have adequate staffing levels on the wards; or
- we are not following the protocol etc.

But the answer in not 'we do not know what to do so we have tested or will test whether treatment A is better or worse than treatment B'. If that is the answer, it was not an audit in the first place because one could not have answered the question 'what should we be doing?' which is the starting point for the audit cycle.

Characteristics of audit and research

The table suggests some characteristics of audit and research. These characteristics lie on a continuum, for example, although the table suggests that audit is less precise than research, generally speaking, some audits are more precise than others and some research is less precise than other research. These characteristics are not foolproof ways of distinguishing audit and research, but are offered for discussion.

Audit	Research
Methodology and design	
Less precise	More precise
Smaller sample sizes	Larger sample sizes
Shorter time scale	Longer time scale
Flexible methodology	Strictly defined methodology
Compares the same activities	Compares different things
Observational	Experimental
Practical/empirical	Theoretical
Uses a Bayesian approach	Uses a frequentist approach
Ethos	
More context specific	Less context specific
Managerial	Scientific
Holistic	Reductionist
Change oriented	Not change oriented
Implementation is essence	Fact is essence
Knowledge for decision making	Knowledge for its own sake
Systems oriented	Not systems oriented
Learning style	
Subjective	Objective
Personal	Impersonal
Experiential	Not experiential

Conclusion

I welcome feedback. For reasons which I have tried to make clear, I think it is in everybody's interests to agree to call things by their proper names. To do this, we have to identify the activities and then agree labels.

CHAPTER TEN

Audit by any other name

Mark Charny

T he previous article discusses how audit might be disting-
uished from research. But it's not just audit and research
which are confused. 'Audit' is a portmanteau word, used
loosely to cover a wide range of activities. Like the word 'health', it
means different things to different people. There are good audits
which have not been called audit, and we commonly see activities
called audit which do not seem like audits. The table overleaf shows
some of these activities, with a brief statement of purpose.

Can you audit outcomes?

In my view, no activity can properly be called an outcome audit. I
am not suggesting that outcomes are unimportant—far from it.
Curing and caring for people is the reason we have a health service,
and any time or money spent on activities which do not help people
to live better and healthier lives is time or money wasted. I share the
concern of most people I speak to that if we are not careful we count
beans: the numbers of people seen in outpatients rather what
happens to them; or the numbers of people on the waiting list

Activity	Purpose
Audit	To establish that we are doing the right things right
Research	To establish what the right things are
Surveillance/ monitoring	To scan key measures of activity or health in order to have early warning of unusually high or low values; finding outlying values triggers local work, usually an audit
Lobbying	To show decision-makers that there is a deficiency, usually of inputs, so that they will provide more resources.
Standards setting	To decide what to do, either on the basis of research evidence or, where this is lacking, by some other means (e.g. consensus), so that all concerned are clear as to objectives and methods
Benchmarking	To compare performance of your unit with similar units to establish either or both of what standards you might expect to achieve or how to achieve those standards.
Baseline survey	To establish the facts at a point in time for either or both of two purposes: as the basis for before/after comparisons or to decide what is achievable locally
Action research	To understand cause and effect relationships using a study design in which the investigator is part of the experiment and the original cause may be altered in the course of the experiment because of feedback from initial results.
Complaints	To study complaints, in order to learn about system failures, with a view to improving future patient care. This may be either surveillance or audit (with the explicit or implicit standard that there should be no complaints)
Establishing user views	To ask patients, users or carers what they want from a service or what they think about it. This may be part of standards setting, or an extension of a complaints system, or part of a diagnostic phase of an audit in which clients are asked to define potential solutions to current problems.
Risk management	To design systems of care in such a way as to minimise risk to patients, with a view to improving care and reducing the potential legal liabilities of an organisation. Audit may be an important component system.
Accreditation	To inspect a pre-determined checklist of inputs (structure) and/or processes, in order to establish an organisation's fitness for purpose.

without taking account of their experience; or the number of tests carried out in a laboratory without any sense of whether they are necessary and useful. But I do not think that it follows from these concerns that one can audit outcomes.

Every 'outcome audit' I have seen is either research or surveillance. The ones which are research compare two (or occasionally more) ways of doing something, and track patients to see what happens to them. The intent of this activity is to decide whether A is better or worse than B in achieving the outcome: this is the answer to the question 'what should we do?', not the answer to the question 'are we doing what we should do?', so it is not audit. In fact, if in such a case we know we should be doing A, we should not compare it with B, since B s by definition a worse treatment and therefore unethical. More commonly, 'outcome audits' are in fact surveillance. They track outcomes in order to see whether the outcomes which should be achieved are in fact being achieved. This looks like the first two stages in the audit cycle: 'we should be achieving this outcome' and 'are we achieving it?', but that is not the same thing as 'we should be doing this and 'are we doing it?'. I am not just splitting hairs here. Suppose for a moment that we can audit outcomes. We establish expected outcomes (for example, from research or benchmarking) and find that the outcomes are not as good as we expect. What comes next? We then need to investigate why this has happened. This looks like stage 3 of the audit cycle, but in fact has moved back to stage 1, 'what should we be doing?'. The only way to influence an outcome is through altering processes, and the only relevant reason why outcomes are not as good as they should be are that care does not conform to those processes. If there are other reasons for poor outcomes, such as local socio-economic factors, these are not under the control of the NHS or local clinicians and it is a cardinal principle of audit that it should address things which are within the power of the participating individuals to alter, otherwise the audit cannot lead to improvements in care with the consequent improvement in outcome which is the purpose of audit. If we already know how local care should be adapted to respond to local factors (for example outreach services, domiciliary family planning etc.) then we already know what processes to track. And if we don't know how local care can help patients to achieve better outcomes, we have to conduct research.

My model for the relationship between audit and outcomes is shown below.

It sees three distinct processes, in which research is an essential bridge between outcomes and audit. Using this approach will make sure that we do not just count beans, and allows audit to concentrate on process improvement which is at the heart of achieving better care for patients.

Outcomes are difficult to measure, for the reasons shown in the table below. But my argument that one cannot audit outcomes has nothing to do with the difficulty of measuring them.

Why outcomes are difficult to measure

May occur much later
May be good with bad care
May be bad with good care
May be due to influences outside the NHS
May be effects of causes decades earlier
May be difficult to define
May be difficult to follow patients

Why has there been so much confusion?

The table overleaf suggest a number of reasons. Compared to research, audit is a very new activity, particularly in health care in the UK. Health care is very complex and what is known about audit and quality improvement largely rests on work in the private rather than the public sector and in less complex manufacturing industries. Because audit is young, methods are still developing. In time, a standard set of robust methodologies will emerge, largely through trial and error, as they have done in research.

Reason	Comment
Methodological uncertainty	Audit is young, methodologies are still emerging
Manipulation	Calling a research project "audit" in order to use an audit budget and/or avoid the problems of ethical approval
Confusion of aims	Lack clarity about the objective of the activity proposed
Overlap of purpose	Some projects have a number of explicit or implicit objectives. This may result in carrying out different activities simultaneously (e.g. using a single data collection form to carry out and audit and research)
Emphasis on data collection	The introduction of audit into the NHS concentrated on an intellectual view of education and data collection; this made audit look like research activity
Misunderstanding	Failure to recognise quality improvement knowledge from outside the health sector and the implications for audit in the NHS
Professional resistance	Seeing audit as about self-regulation and change, often involving many professions and even non-clinical staff, can be challenging personally and to the status of powerful groups

Conclusion

As with audit and research it is important to be clear about any activity so we can be sure that we are using the most appropriate methodology, that the work falls within our remit, and that money is coming from the right budget, and the right people receive reports on the progress and outcome of the project. In distinguishing various activities, I am not seeking to imply that some activities are more important that others. A great variety of work is necessary to improving health care, each making its contribution. To ask whether one activity is more important than another is like asking a carpenter whether a chisel is more important than a hammer. It all depends on what you are trying to do. Being clear about objectives helps and the range of possible methods means that like a good craftsman you can choose the right tool for the job in hand.

PART III:
OUTCOME MONITORING

CHAPTER ELEVEN

Categories of information

Outcome monitoring is not sufficient on its own to tell us how effective our practices are in any meaningful way. To do this we need to collect several types of information routinely—without which, our routine outcome data have no sensible context for their interpretation.

1. Who are the people that use our services?

We need to describe fully the people we treat. Currently, collection of demographic data in psychological treatment services is often restricted to address, date of birth, age, and ethnicity. Other demographic information may appear in session notes but for the most part this information is inaccessible for quick analysis and not in any standardized format. This will need to change in line with the requirements of the NHS Mental Health Minimum Data Set (see Part V).

To report this kind of information, it is useful to have it systematically collected in one place. For an example of an extensive dataset of this sort, see the Association for Child Psychology and

Psychiatry (ACPP) data set developed by Michael Berger *et al.* (1993) for use in Child and Adolescent mental health services.

2. What services do we provide?

To be able to say that what we do is effective, we need to be able to document what it is that we do. Classification systems used by Service Agreements Departments to bill Health Authorities or Primary Care Trusts may not necessarily coincide with a clinical description of what treatments we give to patients. It may be necessary to consider a clinical system of classification alongside this system.

3. What problems do the people who come to us for help present with?

We need to be able to describe the problems that people come to us with if we are to be able to say whether our service has been helpful in a way that will be meaningful to potential referrers or commissioners. Without this information, any positive outcome information we collect could be viewed as be null and void, since the argument might be put that there might have been nothing much wrong in the first place, i.e. that we are seeing only the "worried well".

There are various ways of describing the problems people come with. One approach involves the use of a formal diagnosis, such as those provided by the DSM and ICD systems of classification (American Psychiatric Association, 1994; World Health Organisation, 1996). Another may be in the form of a checklist of problems or symptoms such as the Clinical Features section of the ACPP Data Set or the Clinical Data Form developed from it at the Tavistock Clinic for use on an adult population (see Part V). Yet another approach is to select a validated checklist of problems that is sensitive to change, i.e. can be used pre- and post-intervention (and at various follow-up intervals) as a "broadband" measures of functioning.

EXAMPLES OF GLOBAL MEASURES

- Children: Child Behaviour Checklist (©Achenbach)
- Adolescents/young adults: Youth Self Report Form/Young Adult Report Form (©Achenbach)
- Adults: CORE (©CORE System Group/Mental Health Foundation)

(See Part V section for copies of these instruments.)

4. What is the outcome of treatment?

Once the first three information requirements are met, we are in a position to measure outcomes. However, there are many different ways and various different levels on which to consider the outcome of a psychological treatment.

Symptoms/diagnoses

Perhaps the most obvious level on which to consider outcome is that of symptoms or diagnostic status. It could be said that a successful treatment is one which leads to a reduction or elimination of symptoms. Clear evidence of such an effect would provide a strong case for continued funding of the particular treatment in question.

This is not an uncontentious area, however, and some psychotherapists, especially those of a psychoanalytic or humanistic persuasion, would consider that symptom based measures provide a poor reflection of the potential breadth and depth of the impact of their therapeutic work. The arguments pertaining to this are explored in Roth & Fonagy (1996) as well as in the Richardson paper reproduced in Part I of this volume. In the final analysis, however, and from the perspective of the service user, it might be considered an indictment of any psychotherapeutic approach if no visible symptom-related change could be observed following exposure to psychological therapy.

Since it is relatively easy to identify various physical symptoms, such as swelling, redness, and fever, it is relatively easy to identify when these symptoms have lessened or gone. It would therefore be relatively easy to establish whether a treatment for these symptoms appeared to lead to the elimination or reduction of the symptoms. It is more difficult to establish the presence or absence of psychological symptoms. There are numerous rating scales and diagnostic interviews which can be used to measure psychological symptoms, such as the broadband measures described above, as well as scales more specific to certain conditions such as the Beck Depression Inventory (Beck *et al.*, 1979). Although these scales take a long time to develop, in order to ensure they are reliable and valid, such scales are becoming more widely available and easy to use.

However, in addition to the specific concerns of psychoanalytic and humanistic psychotherapists, there are several general issues surrounding the use of symptom scales to measure outcomes of psychological treatments. For example, symptoms such as low mood and lack of concentration are fairly common and frequently transient. It is only when they are numerous or persist and when they interfere in normal social functioning or with development that we may consider intervention. But how numerous is numerous and how persistent is persistent? Symptom scales often have cut-points to classify the respondent. These need to be based to a certain extent on clinical judgement in order to be clinically relevant. Symptom scales can, therefore, never be as purely scientific as they may appear to be at face value, even though at the level of face value they may provide the most meaningful evidence to most audiences.

Another issue arising from the use of symptom scales is that many psychological symptoms are based on the individual's behaviour, such as sleeping, crying, being restless, acting out. How can one take account of the fact that different observers may report different levels of symptoms in the same individual? For example, Cottrell (1998) states that parents regularly report higher levels of behavioural disturbance and lower levels of emotional distress in their teenage children than do the children themselves. Cottrell therefore asks, "if parents and children disagree, whose outcome is to be measured and/or believed?"

Interpersonal functioning

Another level on which to scrutinize the outcome of a psychological treatment is in terms of interpersonal functioning. This addresses the idea that improving a person's mental health has a wider purpose than merely eliminating their symptoms. It is also important that any treatment has a relevant effect on the individual's life, in terms of their relationships and their general functioning within society, such as being able to work and engage in social activities. Despite the obvious importance of the concept, there are relatively few acceptable measures or even theories of adaptation on which to build such measures. Some general symptom measures include questions about general life functioning (such as the CORE, Evans *et al.*, 2000; see Part V) and there are a number of measures looking at how an individual relates to other people (such as the "Persons relating to others questionnaire", Birtchnell, 1999; and the Inventory of Interpersonal Problems, Horowitz *et al.*, 1988). However, there is a need to consider further how to evaluate the effect of interventions, not just on core symptoms, but on general functioning.

In considering this level of outcome, it may also be important to consider the extent to which certain ideas about psychosocial adaptation are culture-bound. For example, having a poor social network in one culture may be seen as independence in another (DeSantis & Thomas, 1994; Whiteford & Wilcock, 2000).

Health service utilization

This level of outcome evaluates the effectiveness of interventions in reducing later health service utilization; for example, people with psychological problems, such as depression, may visit their general practitioner or other services primarily in order to have contact with a caring professional. A more intensive long-term psychological intervention such as psychotherapy, may be initially more costly but may result in less unnecessary utilization of primary care resources in the long-term.

One problem for the health services in the UK is the potential for some interventions to affect service utilization in other public sector services and the associated difficulty, until recently, of cross departmental funding and evaluation. Thus, interventions funded by the health service may reduce delinquency and affect levels of service utilization in the criminal justice system. Similarly, interventions with children who may have been abused may reduce uptake of social service department resources later or impact on educational services.

A further complication is that an intervention may be designed to increase uptake of appointments, reducing dropout rates or otherwise influencing clients' current and future use of the service. In spite of the obvious complexities involved in measuring the broader and long-term cost-effectiveness of services, health economists have developed measures such as the Client Service Receipt Inventory to be able to look at the overall costs of service use (Beecham & Knapp, 1992).

User satisfaction

There are many patient satisfaction questionnaires, as most surveys of service users' views tend to be based on a questionnaire that the investigators have developed for local purposes and there are few published, validated, and reliable measures. Moreover, there are several methodological problems with measuring patient satisfaction. For example, when respondents are asked a series of direct questions about satisfaction with aspects of services, these may not be the areas which they would themselves give priority to reporting on. It has been suggested that a true user survey would be designed primarily by users themselves, hence a current drive for more "user-led" research and audit rather than simply "user involvement".

There are also problems with the different approaches to measuring satisfaction (see Carr-Hill, 1992). One approach is to have a global evaluation, asking patients simply to rate their overall satisfaction with the service they received. Global evaluations may be inadequate because those who report that they are very satisfied in general will nevertheless articulate specific complaints or criticisms when asked. Another approach is to have several items covering various areas of service provision which make up either one composite measure or several different measures for each aspect of care. Using one composite score is problematic because it assumes that each of the items contributing to it deserves equal weighting and that patients do not have priorities for different aspects of a service. A patient satisfaction survey should, therefore, ideally be developed by and for users, cover a wide range as possible of service areas, allow room for making comments, as well as structured response questions, and, in analysis, treat each item individually at face value. Furthermore, consideration should be given to finding out what user's priorities are and therefore how much weight should be given to satisfaction ratings. See Car-Hill (1992) for more discussion of theoretical and methodological issues in measuring patient satisfaction and see Part IV for more on user involvement in audit and research.

Measuring outcomes

Pre- and post-broadband measures (i.e. assessing multiple domains of functioning, as discussed above) can be used as outcome measures and are useful in that they attempt to cover the broadest possible range of clinical features. These are a good place to start with outcome monitoring. However, you may be interested in more specific areas of functioning. There have been measures developed and validated in many areas, for example depression, anxiety, addiction, coping, stress, quality of life etc. Carry out a literature search in the area you are interested in to find out about measures that have been developed and used in other similar services.

It is increasingly recognized that reliance on a single source of information about clinical outcome is potentially unreliable. Wherever possible a clinician perspective as well as a patient perspective should be obtained. Moreover, it will often be helpful to "triangulate" our assessment of outcome by obtaining information from other sources (e.g. parents, carers, teachers, significant others etc.) For an example of this see the Brandon Centre programme described on page 106.

References

American Psychiatric Association (1994). *Diagnostic and Statistical Manual of Mental Disorders* (4th edn). Washington, D.C.: American Psychiatric Association.

Beck, A. T., Rush, A. J., Shaw, B. F., & Emery, G. (1979). *Cognitive Therapy of Depression*. New York: Guildford Press.

Berger, M. *et al.* (1993). A Proposed Core Data Set for Child and Adolescent Psychology and Psychiatry Services, ACPP.

Birtchnell, J. (1999). *Relating in Psychotherapy: The application of a new theory*. CT, USA: Prager Publishers.

Carr-Hill, R. A. (1992). The measurement of patient satisfaction. *Journal of Public Health Medicine, 14*(3): 236–249.

Cottrell, D. (1998). The use of outcomes in CAMHS, Paper presented to the Royal College of Psychiatrists Research Unit meeting "Developing Effective Child and Adolescent Mental Health Services: current initiatives and innovations", London: Royal College of Physicians, February 1999.

Beecham, J., & Knapp, M. (1992). Client Service Receipt Interview (CSRI)—Costing psychiatric interventions. In: G. Thornicroft, C. R. Brewin & J. Wing (Eds), *Measuring Mental Health Needs*. American Psychiatric Press Inc.

DeSantis, L., & Thomas, J. T. (1994). Childhood independence: Views of Cuban and Haitian immigrant mothers. *Journal of Pediatric Nursing, 9*(4): 258–267.

Evans, C., Mellor Clark, J., Margison, F., Barkham, M., Audin, K., Connell, J., & McGrath, G. (2000). Clinical outcomes in routine evaluation (CORE): A measure of clinical effectiveness and for practice based evidence. *Journal of Mental Health, 3*: 247–255.

Horowitz, L. M., Rosenberg, S. E., Baer, B. A., Ureño, G., & Villaseñor, V. S. (1988). The Inventory of Interpersonal Problems: Psychometric properties and clinical applications. *Journal of Consulting and Clinical Psychology, 56*: 885–895.

World Health Organisation (1996). The ICD-10 Classification of Mental and Behavioural Disorders. Diagnostic Criteria for Research.

Whiteford, G., & Wilcock, A. (2000). Cultural relativism: Occupation and independence reconsidered. *Canadian Journal of Occupational Therapy, 67*(5).

CHAPTER TWELVE

Choosing outcome measures: considerations

W hen thinking about what tools to use for all the types of information described, there are several considerations to take into account. They cannot all be met fully and compromises will always have to be made, since no perfect tool is ever likely to be created. The following is a list of some things you may want to take into account.

Selection of measures

- Using measuring instruments that are meaningful to the therapies practised in this Trust.
- Using measures that are meaningful to service users and external agencies who might ask you for information.
- Are the tools valid and reliable? For what populations are they valid and reliable? E.g. was it validated in the USA or in Britain? Are normative data available for the measure?
- Will the tools measure what you do without substantively altering what you do (i.e. is the measurement reactive)?
- How can cost-effectiveness be evaluated alongside clinical effectiveness?

- Will the tools be self-report, teacher-rated, parent-rated, clinician-rated etc? What are the problems with each of these approaches? How will discrepancies be handled if multiple sources are used?
- Will your tools measure general problems or specific problems such as depression/anxiety?
- If published, are standardized questionnaires and checklists copyrighted, how much do they cost?

Administration of measures

- Instruments may require additional training for staff which will impact on the training systems in place. Using an instrument badly or without sufficient training can be worse than using a simpler instrument sensibly.
- The use of outcome measures will require additional clinician time. Work out how much is manageable and when it should happen.
- When will the tools be administered? On first or second contact or after the assessment, at the end of contact, at follow-up? Note that if a measure is not taken before and after first contact, you may lose evidence of an improvement due simply to anxiety relief resulting from the first contact.
- How will the culture within which you work be altered to allow for this scale of service reorganization?
- How will the tools you use link in with tools being used in other areas of the Trust?
- How will the data be analysed on a regular basis? Can your data be integrated with current computer (patient administration) systems and any future plans for local development of the electronic patient record (EPR)?
- Has informed consent been obtained from service users for eventual publication of results?

EXAMPLE: BRANDON CENTRE EVALUATION OF OUTCOMES (1993 ONWARDS)

Geoffrey Baruch at the Brandon Centre in London has pioneered the use of routine outcome monitoring in the context of outpatient psychodynamic psychotherapy services for young people. The measures standardly employed are detailed below.

Population information

The details of Brandon Centre Patients (demographic, familial, occupational, and educational) were completed by the clinician as the information arose during interviews.

Clinical characteristics at intake

- Global Assessment of Functioning Scale (condensed version of Global Assessment Scale): clinicians rate adolescents level of functioning, according to guidelines, on a scale of 1–100.
- Severity of Psychosocial stressors scale (from Axis IV of DSM-III-R): clinicians rate severity of various stresses on a scale of 1–6.
- Presentation of Problems form: clinician fills out form comprising 39 items.
- ICD-10: an ICD diagnosis and principal diagnosis is assigned following two clinical interviews. Clinicians have been instructed in ICD-10.

Outcome measures (modified versions of Child Behaviour Checklist)

- Youth Self Report Form (11–18)/Young Adult Self Report Form (18–28): young person completes with clinician in first or second interview or independently after first interview and brings to next appointment. Repeated at 3, 6, and 12 months and then 12 monthly.
- Significant Other's Form/Young Adult Behaviour Checklist: given to young person after first interview and asked to have somebody important to them, e.g. parent, boyfriend, fill it in and bring with them to next session. Also completed by clinician. Repeated at same intervals as above.

Managing change

The proposed incorporation into the clinical sphere of work of a self-report form filled out by the young person and a form filled out by a significant other at intake, and then followed up periodically, posed the greatest difficulty for clinical practice. There was a great deal of anxiety, which I shared with the clinical staff, about whether the forms would deter young people from coming to the centre, and how much the forms would interfere with the therapeutic process. There were three matters which helped in the management of change. Firstly because the centre is in the voluntary sector, the staff have a stake in any activity which contributes to the centre's funding. Secondly, I ran a six month pilot study, administering the forms to all my new patients. This was helpful in giving the staff confidence that the forms could be introduced without damaging the therapeutic relationship. The piloting enabled me to learn about the problems of administration, and so develop a procedure based on this experience. Thirdly, the psychotherapists have been permitted a certain flexibility as to how they administer the forms. For instance, some young people are asked to complete the form at home and return it at the next session; whereas others fill in the form during the session. The psychotherapist can exclude young people who are unwilling to participate, or who are unable to fill in the form because they are severely disturbed and in crisis. Since the audit began, only a handful of young people have been excluded on these grounds. Several young people with learning disabilities have been helped by their psychotherapist to read the questions. [Baruch, 1995]

References

Baruch, G. (1995). Evaluating the outcome of a community based psychoanalytic psychotherapy service for young people between 12 and 25 years old: work in progress. *Psychoanalytic Psychotherapy*, 9(3): 241–267.

PART IV:
EVIDENCE BASED PRACTICE

CHAPTER THIRTEEN

Resources for EBP

O ne of the problems for most clinicians is that of obtaining relevant evidence. Published evidence is very disparate and may appear in many different journals or other publication sources and is therefore not easy to find or to find quickly. This makes it very difficult for clinicians to find enough time to keep up with all potentially relevant published research. This has given rise to evidence based journals in which the searching, digesting and categorizing is already done.

Journals/effectiveness reviews

Below is a selection of journals on evidence based practice and effectiveness reviews. Some are available online. See internet section below for web addresses.

- British Journal of Clinical Governance: Original articles relating to audit, evidence based practice, clinical guidelines, risk management and implementation of best practice health outcomes.
- Evidence Based Mental Health: Summaries of research topics for clinicians (online).

- Guidelines in practice: Addresses aspects of guidelines, audit and clinical effectiveness, mainly in primary care.
- Journal of Clinical Excellence: Articles relating to the promotion of clinical excellence.
- Cochrane Systematic Reviews: Systematic reviews of Randomised Controlled Trials (online).
- Effective Health Care bulletins: Centre for Reviews and Dissemination bulletin—summaries of systematic reviews in specific areas (online).
- Health Technology Assessment Reports: Reports on centrally funded original research and systematic reviews on health technologies.
- Clinical Evidence: Summaries of best available evidence on a wide range of subjects based on randomised trials and systematic reviews (online).
- Bandolier: Evidence based summaries (bullet points) (online).

Bibliographic databases

Databases are extremely useful for searching for the available evidence in a particular area. The following table lists some of the available databases and whether they are available only on CD-ROM or through the internet. Most databases available on the internet are only available free to members of licensed institutions, e.g. libraries/higher education and other users need to obtain a username and password from the library. Others are available free without a licence. See the Internet section below for web addresses.

Online

- PsycINFO: Psychological literature from 1887–present.
- E-Psyche: Psychological literature;, should be used in conjunction with PsycINFO.
- Medline: Bio-medical literature.
- British Education Index/Web of Science: Social sciences literature from 1981. Hosts Social Sciences Citation Abstracts and Science Citation Abstracts.
- ERIC: Special needs material, educational psychology as well as normal educational resources.

- The Cochrane Library: Evidence to inform health care decision making (Including: Cochrane Database of Systematic Reviews, Database of Abstracts of Reviews of Effectiveness and the Cochrane Controlled Trials Register) (online).
- CINAHL: Information for Nursing and other health care professions (online).
- Embase: Includes data from 3500 biomedical journals published in 110 countries, dating back to 1980. Updated monthly (online).

CD-ROM

- Bookfind: Information on over 1000,000 titles.
- Assia Plus: Social sciences literature from 1987 including social work.
- ChildData: Covers all aspects of children and young people's welfare, from 1989.
- Caredata: Community and social care database by National Institute for Social Work.
- British Nursing Index: Nursing database 1994–present.
- Ulrich's OnDisc: Ulrich's International Periodical's directory.

Internet

The Internet is an extremely useful resource for Evidence Based Practice. The following sites are particularly useful for Evidence Based Mental Health:

Free bibliographic database services

- PubMed: www.ncbi.nlm.nih.gov/Literature/Index.html
- BioMedNet: journals.bmn.com
- Cochrane Library (abstracts free): www.update-software.com/cochrane/abstract.htm

Information about purchasing CD ROMs or internet licences for bibliographic databases

- BIDS (for ERIC Embase, Medline): www.bids.ac.uk
- Ovid (for Medline, CINAHL, Embase, PsychINFO): www.ovid.com

- Athens (manages access to range of databases): www.athens.ac.uk

Online journals/bulletins

- Evidence Based Mental Health: www.psychiatry.ox.ac.uk/cebmh
- Clinical Evidence: www.evidence.org
- Effective Health care bulletins: www.york.ac.uk/inst/crd/ehcb.htm
- Bandolier: www.jr2.ox.ac.uk/Bandolier
- Attract: www.attract.wales.nhs.uk
- Evidence Based Practice: www.ot.curtin.edu.au
- Evidence Based Care in Mental Health Nursing: www.nursing-standard.co.uk

Organizations/Institutions

- Centre for Outcomes Research and Evaluation: www.psychol.ucl.ac.uk/CORE/home.html
- Kings Fund: www.kingsfund.org.uk
- National Electronic Library for Mental Health: www.nelmh.org
- Cochrane Collaboration: www.update-software.com/collaboration
- Centre for Evidence Based Mental Health: www.cebmh.com
- National Institute for Clinical Excellence: www.nice.org.uk/nice-web
- Centre for Reviews and Dissemination: www.york.ac.uk/inst/crd/welcome.htm
- Royal College of Psychiatrists College Research Unit: www.rcpsych.ac.uk/cru/
- College of Health: www.collegeofhealth.org.uk
- Centre for Evidence Based Child Health: www.ich.ucl.ac.uk/ebm/ebm.htm

Other websites particularly related to clinical guidelines are also given in Clinical Guidelines, Chapter Fourteen.

National Institute for Clinical Excellence (NICE)

Plans for NICE were set out in the 1998 White Paper, "A First Class Service". It came into being as a Special Health Authority on 1st April 1999. Its main functions are:

- appraisal of new and existing technologies;
- development of clinical guidelines; and
- production and dissemination of clinical audit methodologies and information on good practice.

To carry out the last function, NICE has absorbed the NCCA (National Centre for Clinical Audit). Until the NCCA was absorbed by NICE, it acted as an accessible resource for advice and information for clinical audit departments including:

- bibliographic database (access to grey and published literature on clinical audit, quality improvement and related subjects);
- Audit Index (a national database of audits);
- contacts database (contact details of people and organizations willing to give help and advice for audit and related areas).

These services are still available from NICE and can be found on the NICE website given above. For more information about NICE, read "A First Class Service" or go to the Department of Health website www.doh.gov.uk. Also see Clinical Guidelines, Chapter Fourteen.

The Commission for Healthcare Audit and Inspection (CHAI)

The Commission for Health Improvement was recently replaced by CHAI as of April 2002 and incorporated also the National Care Standards Commission's responsibilities for inspecting the private health sector and the Audit Commission's "value for money" studies in health. CHAI/CHI continues to conduct reviews that assess clinical governance implementation within a trust, evaluating clinical governance by exploring three key areas.

1. "Strategic capacity": how far does the trust's leadership set a clear overall direction that focuses on patients? How well is it integrated throughout the trust?

2. "Resources and processes": how robust are its processes for achieving quality improvement, such as consultation and patient involvement and clinical audit?
3. "Use of information": what information is available on patient's experience, outcomes, processes, and resources, and how does the trust use it strategically and at the level of patient care?

A trust's performance in these areas is evaluated on a four-point scale assessing each component of the three above named areas. Detailed reports are published on the internet in an attempt to spread learning to the widest audience possible and CHAI will continue to post documents on the same address at http://www.chi.nhs.uk

Search Strategies for Bibliographic Databases

The manner in which searches of CD-ROM or internet reference databases are carried out can determine what is found. Without a search strategy the search may not retrieve all the relevant articles in the database. Expert search strategies can be developed for those who wish to carry out comprehensive searches for reviewing an area. The following examples are strategies for identifying randomized controlled trials of cognitive therapy for depression. The databases used are Embase, Medline and PsycINFO.

The examples are taken from: Watson R. & Richardson P. (1999), Identifying randomised controlled trials of cognitive therapy for depression: Comparing the efficiency of Embase, Medline, and PsycINFO bibliographic databases (Appendix), *British Journal of Medical Psychology*, 72.

Standard Search Strategies (Index terms only)

Embase Strategy	Medline Strategy	PsycINFO Strategy
treatment outcome/	randomised controlled trial.pt	treatment effectiveness evaluation/
major clinical study/	random allocation/	exp treatment outcomes
randomised controlled trial/	double blind method/	psychotherapeutic outcomes/
randomisation/	single blind method/	placebo/
double blind procedure/	treatment outcomes/	follow up studies/
single blind procedure/	follow up studies/	cognitive therapy/
placebo/	clinical trial.pt/	cognitive techniques/
methodology/	placebos/	cognitive restructuring/

Embase Strategy	Medline Strategy	PsycINFO Strategy
comparison/	(animal non (human and animal)).sh.	major depression/
follow up/	cognitive therapy/	affective disturbances/
prospective study/	depression/	
cognitive therapy/	depressive disorder	
depression/	affective disorders	
affective neurosis/		

Expert Search Strategies (Index plus free text/truncated search terms)

Embase Strategy	Medline Strategy	PsycINFO Strategy
treatment outcome/	randomised controlled trial.pt	treatment effectiveness evaluation/
major clinical study/	random allocation/	exp treatment outcomes
randomised controlled trial/	double blind method/	psychotherapeutic outcomes/
randomisation/	single blind method/	placebo/
double blind procedure/	treatment outcomes/	follow up studies/
single blind procedure/	follow up studies/	placebo$.tw.
placebo/	clinical trial.pt/	random$.tw.
methodology/	placebos/	comparativ stud$.tw.
comparison/	(clin$ adj3 trial$).tw.	randomi#ed controlled trial$.tw.
follow up/	((singl$ or doubl$ or trebl$ or tripl$) adj3 (blind$ or mask$)).tw.	(clinical adj3 trial$).tw.
prospective study/	randomi#ed controlled trial$.tw	(research adj3 design).tw.
randomi#ed controlled trial$.tw.	placebo$.tw.	(evaluat$ adj3 stud$).tw.
(clin$ adj3 trial$).tw.	random$.tw.	(prospectiv$ adj3 stud$).tw.
((singl$ or doubl$ or trebl$ or tripl$) adj3 (blind$ or mask$))	comparative stud$.tw.	((singl$ or doubl$ or trebl$ or tripl$) adj3 (blind$ or mask$)).tw.
placebo$.tw.	(evaluat$ adj3 stud$).tw.	cognitive therapy/
random$.tw.	(prospectiv$ adj3 stud$).tw.	cognitive techniques/
(control$ or prospectiv$ or volunteer$).tw.	(contro$ or prospectiv$ or volunteer$).tw.	cognitive restructuring/
(research adj3 design).tw.	(research adj3 design).tw.	(cognitive adj therap$).tw.
comparative stud$.tw.	(animal non (human and animal)).sh.	cognitive behavio$ therap$.tw.
(evaluat$ adj3 stud).tw.	cognitive therapy/	cbt.tw.
prospect$ adj3 stud$).tw.	(cognitive adj therap$).tw.	major depression/
cognitive therapy/	cognitive behavio$ therap$.tw.	affective disturbances/
(cognitive adj therap$).tw.	cbt.tw.	depress$.tw.
cognitive behavio$ therap$.tw.	depression/	(affective adj dis$).tw.
cbt.tw	depressive disorder/	(mood adj dis$).tw.
depression/	affective disorders/	

Embase Strategy	Medline Strategy	PsycINFO Strategy
affective neurosis/	depress$.tw.	
depress$.tw	(affective adj dis$).tw.	
(affective adj dis$).tw.	(mood adj dis$).tw.	
(mood adj dis$).tw.		

Libraries in London

Below is a selection of London libraries particularly useful for finding information and evidence on psychotherapy, psychology, psychiatry and social work, many of which provide access to the databases listed above. Outside London, local university or hospital libraries should also be useful sources for journals and databases.

- Tavistock Library (www.tavi-port.org): Available to Tavistock and Portman staff and students (Visitors pay fee). Holds a wide range of books and journals mainly in fields of Psychiatry, Psychology, Psychoanalysis, Forensic Psychotherapy, Educational Psychology, Clinical Psychology, Organizational Psychology and Social Work (Tavistock Centre, 120 Belsize Lane, London NW3 5BA. Tel.: 020-7447-3732; Fax: 020-7447-3734).
- Health Promotion Library and Information Centre: Available to anyone living or working in Camden or Islington. Databases: Helpbox, Patientwise, Drugdata, Cochrane Library (St. Pancras Hospital, 4 St. Pancras Way, London NW1 0PE. Tel.: 020-7530-3910; Fax: 020-7530-3904).
- King's Fund Library and Information Service (www.kingsfund. org.uk): Reference only. Wide-ranging collection including mental health; especially good on nursing and health service management journals (11–13 Cavendish Square, London, W1M 0AN. Tel.: 020-7307-2568; Fax: 020-7307-2806).
- British Library (www.bl.uk): Holds databases not otherwise available in local libraries. Reading Room for official publications and social sciences (Great Russell Street, London WC1 3DG. Tel.: 020-7412-7536).
- Institute of Child Health Library and Resource Centre (www.ich.ucl.ac.uk/library/libguide.htm): Reference only, NHS only; by appointment (Institute of Child Health, 30 Guilford Street, London WC1N 1EH. Tel.: 020-7242-9789).

- University of London Library at Senate House (www.ull.ac.uk/ull): Available to University of London graduates and Members of British Psychological Society; holds the BPS Collection of periodicals (Malet Street, London WC1E 7HY. Tel.: 020-7862-8500; Fax: 020-7862-8480).
- Royal Society of Medicine Library (www.roysocmed.ac.uk/librar/page6.htm): Available to Members of the RSM (1 Wimpole Street, London W1M 8AE. Tel.: 020-7290-2940; Fax: 020-7290-2939).
- British Medical Association Library (library.bma.org.uk): Holds the NICE Clinical Audit Collection; available to BMA members (BMA House, Tavistock Square, London WC1H 9JP. Tel.: 020-7383-6494).
- Institute of Psychiatry Library (www.iop.kcl.ac.uk/IoP/AdminSup/Library/index.stm): Extensive collection of psychiatric and psychological journals; more on behavioural and cognitive therapies than Tavistock Library (De Crespigny Park, London SE5 8AF. Tel.: 020-7919-3204; Fax: 020-7703-4515).

CHAPTER FOURTEEN

Clinical guidelines

"Treatment Choice in Psychological Therapies and Counselling"
(DOH, 2001)

T his is an evidence based clinical practice guideline developed to aid decisions about which forms of psychological therapy, currently available in the NHS, are most appropriate for particular patients. The guideline considers which other factors need to be taken into consideration when choosing the most appropriate therapy and has been produced by a multi-disciplinary development group, led by the British Psychological Society and has undergone extensive independent scientific review. The guideline is aimed at GPs and other referring agencies and provides them with clinical guidance on whether and when to refer a patient to counselling or psychological therapies.

The scope of the guideline covers depression, anxiety, post traumatic disorders, obsessive disorders, and personality disorders, as well as chronic pain, chronic fatigue, gastrointestinal disorders, and gynaecological presentations. The types of therapy addressed in the guideline include cognitive behavioural therapy, psychoanalytic therapies, systemic therapy, eclectic therapies, and integrative therapy, among others.

The guideline's approach to identifying and interpreting evidence is from systematic meta-analytic reviews and supplementary searches for missed reviews and individual high quality trials that missed meta-analysis or had not yet been published. A panel of mental health service users was assembled to be involved in the discussions by inviting UK Advocacy Network, Depression Alliance, MIND, and the Centre for Health Information Quality to nominate representatives.

The limitations in the use of the Guideline include gaps in scientific evidence which underpin the recommendations in that a lack of evidence does not identify a type of therapy as less effective than one for which there is much evidence. It should also be noted that much of the evidence informing the Guideline derives from what are now commonly referred to as "efficacy studies". These are typically randomized controlled trials carried out on highly selected patient samples and in ways which make them atypical of routine clinical practice (researcher enthusiasm, frequent and extensive monitoring of patient status, unusually close supervision of the clinical work, etc.). The guideline states that the recommendations are made for therapies for which there is best evidence of efficacy. Many questions remain about the generalizability of findings from such studies to the effectiveness of routine clinical practice and there is increasing recognition of the need for "on-the-ground" "effectiveness" studies to complement what has been learnt from the efficacy research.

> If good quality guidelines exist, there remains controversy over how they are used. Ideally, guidelines crystallise and summarise "best practice" and are used by practitioners to help them make good decisions. They do not replace individual clinical judgement, but provide the means for a better-informed judgement. In being aware of the guideline recommendation, clinicians can choose to do something else. Indeed, as a guideline speaks only of generalities, inevitably there will be individual circumstances where the clinician should choose to do something else. This is why the over-prescriptive use of guidelines is not in the spirit of evidence-based practice and should be discouraged. [Glenys Parry, Chair of the Guidelines Development Group, 2000]

See Part V for a list of the principal recommendations of the guideline.

Other existing guidelines

There are many other existing guidelines relating to mental health. The Royal College of Psychiatrists provides information on guidelines in mental health and the following web address provides links to other mental health related guideline sites: http://www.psychiatry. ox.ac.uk/cebmh/guidelines/

It is never worthwhile developing a guideline locally unless you have first looked to see what already exists. National guidance will be easier to locate than in the past by contacting NICE. National Service Frameworks may also be relevant and NICE will be producing guidelines to support these. The National Collaborating Centre for Mental Health is one of the six collaborating centres established by NICE and is responsible for producing guidelines in relation to mental health. This is a joint project between the College Research Unit (CRU) of the Royal College of Psychiatrists' and the British Psychological Society's Clinical Effectiveness Unit (CORE). For information about guidelines developed or in development at the Centre, see their website at www.rcpsych.ac.uk/cru/nccmh.htm.

> A useful principle is never develop your own guideline unless there is really no alternative. Developing a guideline takes a lot of time and skill. If there are no existing guidelines or the existing guidelines are not of adequate quality it may be because the subject area is difficult and complex to deal with or because there is a lack of evidence on the subject. You may either want to modify existing guidelines or take on the development of a guideline. If the latter is the only possibility, you could also consider interesting a national organisation [such as the British Psychological Society] to take on the work or support you in it. [Charny, 1999a,b]

Guideline related internet sites

- Database of Critically Appraised Guidelines: From the Institute of Health Sciences in Oxford. Includes a range of high quality guidelines developed locally and nationally across a broad range of topics. Provides an abstract, appraisal and link to full text. (www.ihs.ox.ac.uk/guidelines).
- Royal College of Psychiatrists: Information on guidelines in mental health and a variety of locally produced systematic guides and links to other mental health related guideline sites (www.psychiatry.ok.ac.uk/cebmh/guidelines)

- Centre for Outcomes Research and Evaluation (CORE): CORE is involved in developing guidelines with the National Collaborating Centre for Mental Health. (www.psychol.ucl.ac.uk/CORE/nccmh.html)
- Aggressive Research Intelligence Facility (ARIF): www.bham.ac.uk/arif/.
- Scottish Intercollegiate Guidelines Network (SIGN): www.sign.ac.uk
- Agency for Healthcare Policy and Research (AHCPR): Established as part of the US Department of Health and Human Services (www.ahcpr.gov/).
- National Guideline Clearing-house: US NCG is a comprehensive database of evidence-based clinical practice guidelines and related documents. (www.guideline.gov/).
- National Institute for Clinical Excellence (NICE): NHS body charged with establishing guidance on best practice in relation to drugs, treatments and services. Provides project news and appraisals (www.nice.org.uk/).
- Turning Research into Practice (TRIP): An internet search service that covers a wide range of UK and US clinical effectiveness resources and evidence-based guidelines (www.tripdatabase.com).

References

Charny, M. (1999a). How to find out about existing guidelines. *Guidelines*, 2 May: 58–61.

Charny, M. (1999b). How to draw up your own guidelines. *Guidelines*, 2 July: 59–61.

DOH (2001). Treatment choice guidelines in psychological therapies and counselling. NHS Executive.

Parry, G. (2000). Treatment choice guidelines in psychotherapy. *Journal of Mental Health*, 9(3): 273–281.

CHAPTER FIFTEEN

Involving health service users

S ince 1994, the Department of Health has encouraged NHS health care providers to address the issue of involving heath service users in clinical audit. The new independent body, "Voice" sets national standards and monitors local services helping to ensure communities have an effective say in their local NHS. Voice has been established to work alongside the trust-based Patients Forums and the Patient Advisory and Liaison Services. The aim is to promote a culture of partnership between health care providers and the consumer, ensuring that clinical care provided is effective and results in the best outcome, from a joint perspective, rather than from the health care professionals' perspective alone. This is now one of the central planks of NHS policy as laid down in the National Service Framework for mental health.

Seeking user involvement aims to ensure:

- that guidelines and standards developed are acceptable to patients and lead to a mutually satisfactory outcome;
- that any changes made to care provision are acceptable;
- that patients are empowered to share in the responsibility for decisions about their care and informed decision making is promoted;

- that health care providers are accountable for the care they provide;
- that a culture of collaboration, good communication and openness is created; and
- that health care professionals and users are educated in the process.

Who should be involved in audit?

When planning a quality improvement project, it may be relevant to involve the following users of health services.

- People who are currently patients or clients
- People who have been patients or clients in the past
- People from ethnic minority groups
- Representatives from Community Health Councils
- User/carer organizations (MIND, the Patient's Association, local User Groups)

You may wish to set up a User Group for your service. This may take the form of a reference group to consult on various issues, or it may take the form of a support group or both. It is important to remember that the group is mainly for the benefit of the "users" and therefore the eventual form it may take should be left to be shaped by the users themselves.

Further reading

Avis, M. (1997). Incorporating patients' voices in the audit process. *Quality in Health Care*, 6: 86–89.

Judd, M. (1997). A pragmatic approach to user involvement in clinical audit—making it happen. *Journal of Clinical Effectiveness*, 2(2): 35–38.

McClelland, F. (1998). MIND's policy on User Involvement. Monitoring our services ourselves. *Mental Health Care*, 1(8): 272–274.

Royal College of Psychiatrists (1999). Consumerism in Mental Health, Conference Abstracts.

Stevenson, K. (1997). Warm soft fuzzies? Is there a problem involving patients in audit? *Audit Trends*, 5 March.

PART V:
APPENDIX

Audit Project Form[1]

Date:

This form has been designed to 1) help compile a database of all audit work going on in the Trust which will inform Annual Audit Reports; 2) help in the thinking about and planning of an audit project and 3) indicate any support needed. If you are planning or currently undertaking a project or study aimed at evaluating any aspect of clinical work or service delivery, please enter the details of the project on this form and return it to . . .

Department: _____

Unit/Service: _____

What is the title or the topic of the project?

What standards will you be auditing?

a) National professionally agreed standards ☐ Specify: _____

b) No national standards, therefore internally ☐ Specify: _____
   agreed standards

c) No national or internal standards, project will ☐
   develop standards for this area

What aspects of quality/quality domain(s) does the project address?

Equity/Access ☐
Acceptability ☐
Appropriateness ☐
Effectiveness ☐
Efficiency ☐
Communication ☐
Continuity ☐

What service area does the project address?

Structure ☐
Process ☐
Outcome ☐

What is the data source for the project?

Routinely collected data ☐
Specific questionnaire/survey ☐

Other: _____

_____

[1] Developed by Susan McPherson for use at the Tavistock & Portman NHS Trust.

Is the data to be audited:	**retrospective** ☐	**or prospective?** ☐

Time period to be audited:	_____ Start date: _____

After how long do you plan to re-audit?

_____

Who will be involved in the audit?

Lead: _____   Profession: _____

Investigator: _____   Profession: _____

Investigator: _____   Profession: _____

Please indicate which stages of the audit cycle the project has been through and what stage it is currently at:

```
          Re-audit ☐                    Set standards ☐

                        AUDIT
                        CYCLE           Collect data ☐
   Implement change ☐

                              Compare practice against standards ☐

   Identify opportunity for improvement ☐
```

Current stage: _____

What change(s) may be or have been made as a result of the audit?

Change to clinical practice (e.g. assessment, treatment)   ☐
Change to organisational process (e.g. waiting times, information recording)   ☐
Change to guidelines/standards   ☐

Other: _____ _____

Was or will a report be produced?

Yes ☐   Expected date of completion: _____
No ☐

Indicate areas in which you would like or have had support with the project:

Project design   ☐
Project management   ☐
Data collection   ☐
Data analysis   ☐
Implementing change   ☐

Other: _____

Please describe any problems you have encountered or anticipate in carrying out the audit:

Thank you for completing this form. Please return it to _____.
If you would like to discuss any aspects of the project before completing the form,
contact _____ *in room* _____ *or extension* _____
or by email (_____ @ _____ *) to arrange a meeting.*

Tavistock and Portman
Clinical Data Form[1]

Please tick as many items as required to cover differing aspects of the clinical presentation, and then identify the patient's three problems by circling.

1 Cognition and Psychological Development	Memory Problems	[ ]
	Attention/Concentration Problems	[ ]
	Confusion/Disorientation	[ ]
	General Learning Disability	[ ]
	Specific LearningDifficulty	[ ]
	Speech Delay/Disorder	[ ]
	Gifted	[ ]
2 Psychosis Type Characteristics	Feelings of Persecution/Harrassment	[ ]
	Unusual/Bizarre Behaviour	[ ]
	Psychotic Symptoms	[ ]
	Autistic Features	[ ]
3 Mood	Irritability/Moodiness	[ ]
	Boredom/Apathy/Fatigue	[ ]
	Low Self Esteem	[ ]
	Depression/Misery	[ ]
	Suicidal Ideation	[ ]
	Euphoria/Expansive Disinhibition	[ ]
	Mood Swings	[ ]
4 Neurotic, Stress Related and Somatoform	Anxiety	[ ]
	Phobias	[ ]
	Obsessions/Compulsions/Rituals	[ ]
5 Self-regulation	Tics/Sterotypies	[ ]
	Habits (incl Lying, Gambling)	[ ]
	Enuresis/Wetting	[ ]
	Soiling/Constipation	[ ]
	Sleep/Waking problems	[ ]
	Problems During Sleep	[ ]
	Overactivity	[ ]
	Anorexia Nervosa	[ ]
	Other eating problems	[ ]
	Substance abuse	[ ]
6 Social and Interpersonal Relationships	Relationship Difficulty With Other Adults	[ ]
	Relationship Difficulty with other Children/Adolescents	[ ]
	Parent/Carer-Child/Adolescent Relationship Difficulty	[ ]
	Marital/Couple Difficulties	[ ]
	Family Relationship Problems	[ ]
	Litigation/Grievance	[ ]

---

[1] Developed by Davenhill, R. and Patrick, M. (based on Berger, M. *et al.*, 1993, A Proposed Core Data Set for Child and Adolescent Psychology and Psychiatry Services, Association of Child Psychology and Psychiatry).

	"Attention-Seeking" Behaviour	[ ]
	Social/Interpersonal Sensitivity	[ ]
	Social Isolation/Withdrawal/Elective mutism	[ ]
7 Self-harm/Injury	Overdose/Suicidal Behaviour	[ ]
	Self Harm/Self-Injurious Behaviour	[ ]
	Risk-Taking	[ ]
8 Anti-Social	Impulsive Behaviour/Tantrums/Outbursts	[ ]
	Non-Compliance/Oppositional Behaviour	[ ]
	Lying	[ ]
	Running Away/wandering	[ ]
	Thieving	[ ]
	Aggressive Behaviour/Fighting/Bullying	[ ]
	Cruelty/Violent Brutality	[ ]
	Firesetting or Destruction of Property	[ ]
9 Sexual and Sex-related	Sexual Dysfunction	[ ]
	Gender Identity Problem	[ ]
	Sexual Preference Problem	[ ]
	Sexual Misdemeanour/Offence	[ ]
	Promiscuity/Use of Prostitutes/Prostitution	[ ]
	Excessive Masturbation/Use of Pornography	[ ]
	Concern about Sexuality	[ ]
	Inappropriately Sexualised Behaviour	[ ]
10 Education/Occupation	Underachievement	[ ]
	Absenteeism/Dropping Out	[ ]
	School Refusal/Phobia	[ ]
	Reactions to severe stress	[ ]
	Adjustment Reaction	[ ]
	Physical symptoms of preoccupations	[ ]
	Fictitious Illness	[ ]
	Hysteria/Conversion	[ ]
11 Abuse/Neglect	Victim of Child Sexual Abuse	[ ]
	Victim of Child Abuse Physical/Emotional (incl neglect)	[ ]
	Failure to Thrive	[ ]
	Agent of Child Sexual Abuse	[ ]
	Agent of Child Abuse Physical/Emotional	[ ]
	Victim of Persecution/Torture	[ ]
12 Context	Adverse Personal/Social Circumstances	[ ]
	Past History of Mental Health Problems	[ ]
	Physical Illness/Disability	[ ]
	Family Mental Health Problems	[ ]
	Family Physical Health Problems	[ ]
	Significant Law Breaking	[ ]
	Court Involvement	[ ]

CONSIDERING THE OVERALL CLINICAL PRESENTATION, PLEASE RATE THE FOLLOWING (see glossary for advice on scoring):

Severity of functional impairment	1	2	3
Chronicity of main problems	1	2	3
Complexity of difficulties 1	2	3	

ICD-10 DIAGNOSIS AND CODE (optional)

Child Behaviour Checklist (sample form)

CHILD BEHAVIOUR CHECKLIST FOR AGES 6-18

Below is a list of items that describe children and youth. For each item that describes your child now or within the past 6 months, please circle the 2 if the item is very true or often true of your child. Circle the 1 if the item is somewhat or sometimes true of your child. If the item is not true of your child, circle the 0. Please answer all items as well as you can, even if some do not seem to apply to your child.

0 = Not True (as far as you know)   1 = Somewhat or Sometimes True   2 = Very True or Often True

0 1 2 1. Acts too young for his/her age	0 1 2 32. Feels he/she has to be perfect
0 1 2 2. Drinks alcohol without parents' approval (describe):_____	0 1 2 33. Feels or complains that no one loves him/her
	0 1 2 34. Feels others are out to get him/her
_____	0 1 2 35. Feels worthless or inferior
0 1 2 3. Argues a lot	
0 1 2 4. Fails to finish things he/she starts	0 1 2 36. Gets hurt a lot, accident-prone
	0 1 2 37. Gets in many fights
0 1 2 5. There is very little he/she enjoys	
0 1 2 6. Bowel movements outside toilet	0 1 2 38. Gets teased a lot
	0 1 2 39. Hangs around with others who get in trouble
0 1 2 7. Bragging, boasting	
0 1 2 8. Can't concentrate, can't pay attention for long	0 1 2 40. Hears sounds or voices that aren't there (describe):_____
0 1 2 9. Can't get his/her mind off certain thoughts; obsessions (describe):_____	
	0 1 2 41. Impulsive or acts without thinking
_____	0 1 2 42. Would rather be alone than with others
0 1 2 10. Can't sit still, restless, or hyperactive	0 1 2 43. Lying or cheating
0 1 2 11. Clings to adults or too dependent	
0 1 2 12. Complains of loneliness	0 1 2 44. Bites fingernails
	0 1 2 45. Nervous, high strung, or tense
0 1 2 13. Confused or seems to be in a fog	
0 1 2 14. Cries a lot	0 1 2 46. Nervous movements or twitching (describe):
0 1 2 15. Cruel to animals	_____
0 1 2 16. Cruelty, bullying, or meanness to others	0 1 2 47. Nightmares
0 1 2 17. Day-dreams or gets lost in is/her thoughts	0 1 2 48. Not liked by other kids
0 1 2 18. Deliberately harms self or attempt suicide	0 1 2 49. Constipated, doesn't move bowels
0 1 2 19. Demands a lot of attention	0 1 2 50. Too fearful or anxious
0 1 2 20. Destroys his/her own things	0 1 2 51. Feels dizzy or lightheaded
0 1 2 21. Destroys things belonging to his/her family or others	0 1 2 52. Feels too guilty
0 1 2 22. Disobedient at home	0 1 2 53. Overeating
0 1 2 23. Disobedient at school	0 1 2 54. Overtired without good reason
0 1 2 24. Doesn't eat well	0 1 2 55. Overweight
0 1 2 25. Doesn't get along with other kids	56. Physical problems *without known medical cause:*
0 1 2 26. Doesn't seem to feel guilty after misbehaving	0 1 2 a. Aches or pains (not headaches)
0 1 2 27. Easily jealous	0 1 2 b. Headaches
0 1 2 28. Breaks rules at home, school, or elsewhere	0 1 2 c. Nausea, feels sick
0 1 2 29. Fears certain animals, situations, or places, other than school (describe):_____	0 1 2 d. Problems with eyes (describe):_____
	_____
_____	0 1 2 e. Rashes or other skin problems
0 1 2 30. Fears going to school	0 1 2 f. Stomachaches or cramps
	0 1 2 g. Vomiting, throwing up
0 1 2 31. Fears he/she might think or do something bad	0 1 2 h. Other (describe):_____
	_____

Be sure you answered all items. Then see other side

0 = Not True (as far as you know)   **1 = Somewhat or Sometimes True**   **2 = Very True or Often True**

0 1 2	57.	Physically attacks people
0 1 2	58.	Picks nose, skin, or other parts of body (describe):_____
0 1 2	59.	Plays with own sex parts in public
0 1 2	60.	Plays with own sex parts too much
0 1 2	61.	Poor school work
0 1 2	62.	Poorly coordinated or clumsy
0 1 2	63.	Prefers being with older kids
0 1 2	64.	Prefers being with younger kids
0 1 2	65.	Refuses to talk
0 1 2	66.	Repeats certain acts over and over; compulsions (describe):_____
0 1 2	67.	Runs away from home
0 1 2	68.	Screams a lot
0 1 2	69.	Secretive, keeps things to self
0 1 2	70.	Sees things that aren't there (describe):_____
0 1 2	71.	Self-conscious or easily embarrassed
0 1 2	72.	Sets fires
0 1 2	73.	Sexual problems (describe):_____
0 1 2	74.	Showing off or clowning
0 1 2	75.	Too shy or timid
0 1 2	76.	Sleeps less than most kids
0 1 2	77.	Sleeps more than most kids during day and/or night (describe):_____
0 1 2	78.	Inattentive or easily distracted
0 1 2	79.	Speech problem (describe):_____
0 1 2	80.	Stares blankly
0 1 2	81.	Steals at home
0 1 2	82.	Steals outside the home
0 1 2	83.	Stores things up he/she doesn't need (describe): _____

0 1 2	84.	Strange behaviour (describe):_____
0 1 2	85.	Strange ideas (describe):_____
0 1 2	86.	Stubborn, sullen, or irritable
0 1 2	87.	Sudden changes in mood or feelings
0 1 2	88.	Sulks a lot
0 1 2	89.	Suspicious
0 1 2	90.	Swearing or obscene language
0 1 2	91.	Talks about killing self
0 1 2	92.	Talks or walks in sleep (describe):_____
0 1 2	93.	Talks too much
0 1 2	94.	Teases a lot
0 1 2	95.	Temper tantrums or hot temper
0 1 2	96.	Thinks about sex too much
0 1 2	97.	Threatens people
0 1 2	98.	Thumb-sucking
0 1 2	99.	Smokes, chews, or sniffs tobacco
0 1 2	100.	Trouble sleeping (describe):_____
0 1 2	101.	Truancy, skips school
0 1 2	102.	Underactive, slow moving, or lacks energy
0 1 2	103.	Unhappy, sad or depressed
0 1 2	104.	Unusually loud
0 1 2	105.	Uses drugs for nonmedical purposes (**don't** include alcohol or tobacco) (describe):_____
0 1 2	106.	Vandalism
0 1 2	107.	Wets self during the day
0 1 2	108.	Wets the bed
0 1 2	109.	Whining
0 1 2	110.	Wishes to be of opposite sex
0 1 2	111.	Withdrawn, doesn't get involved with others
0 1 2	112.	Worries
	113.	Please write in any problems your child has that were not listed above
0 1 2		_____
0 1 2		_____
0 1 2		_____

PLEASE BE SURE YOU HAVE ANSWERED ALL ITEMS

Youth Self Report (sample form)

YOUTH SELF REPORT FORM FOR AGES 11-18

Below is a list of items that describe children and youth. For each item that describes you now or within the past 6 months, please circle the 2 if the item is very true or often true of you. Circle the 1 if the item is somewhat or sometimes true of you. If the item is not true of you, circle the 0.

0 = Not True (as far as you know)	1 = Somewhat or Sometimes True	2 = Very True or Often True

0 1 2	1. I act too young for my age		0 1 2	33.	I feel that no one loves me
0 1 2	2. I drink alcohol without my parents' approval (describe)_____		0 1 2	34.	I feel that others are out to get me
	_____		0 1 2	35.	I feel worthless or inferior
			0 1 2	36.	I accidentally get hurt a lot
0 1 2	3. I argue a lot		0 1 2	37.	I get in many fights
0 1 2	4. I fail to finish things that I start		0 1 2	38.	I get teased a lot
0 1 2	5. There is very little that I enjoy		0 1 2	39.	I hang around with others who get in trouble
0 1 2	6. I like animals				
0 1 2	7. I brag		0 1 2	40.	I hear sounds or voices that other people think aren't there (describe):_____
0 1 2	8. I have trouble concentrating or paying attention				_____
0 1 2	9. I can't get my mind off certain thoughts; (describe):_____				_____
	_____		0 1 2	41.	I act without stopping to think
			0 1 2	42.	I would rather be alone than with others
0 1 2	10. I have trouble sitting still				
0 1 2	11. I'm too dependent on adults		0 1 2	43.	I lie or cheat
0 1 2	12. I feel lonely		0 1 2	44.	I bite my fingernails
0 1 2	13. I feel confused or in a fog		0 1 2	45.	I am nervous or tense
0 1 2	14. I cry a lot		0 1 2	46.	Parts of my body twitch or make nervous movements (describe):
0 1 2	15. I am pretty honest				_____
0 1 2	16. I am mean to others				_____
0 1 2	17. I daydream a lot				
0 1 2	18. I deliberately try to hurt or kill myself		0 1 2	47.	I have nightmares
			0 1 2	48.	I am not liked by other kids
0 1 2	19. I try to get a lot of attention				
0 1 2	20. I destroy my own things		0 1 2	49.	I can do certain things better than most kids
0 1 2	21. I destroy things belonging to others		0 1 2	50.	I am too fearful or anxious
0 1 2	22. I disobey my parents		0 1 2	51.	I feel dizzy or lightheaded
0 1 2	23. I disobey at school		0 1 2	52.	I feel too guilty
0 1 2	24. I don't eat as well as I should		0 1 2	53.	I eat too much
0 1 2	25. I don't get along with other kids		0 1 2	54.	I feel overtired without good reason
0 1 2	26. I don't feel guilty after doing something I shouldn't		0 1 2	55.	I am overweight
				56.	Physical problems without known medical cause:
0 1 2	27. I am jealous of others		0 1 2	a.	Aches or pains (not stomach or headaches)
0 1 2	28. I break rules at home, school or elsewhere		0 1 2	b.	Headaches
			0 1 2	c.	Nausea, feel sick
0 1 2	29. I am afraid of certain animals, situations, or places, other than school (describe):_____		0 1 2	d.	Problems with eyes (not if corrected by glasses) (describe):_____
	_____		0 1 2	e.	Rashes or other skin problems
			0 1 2	f.	Stomachaches
0 1 2	30. I am afraid of going to school		0 1 2	g.	Vomiting, throwing up
0 1 2	31. I am afraid I might think or do something bad		0 1 2	h.	Other (describe):_____
0 1 2	32. I feel that I have to be perfect				

Be sure you answered all items. Then see other side

0 = Not True (as far as you know)   1 = Somewhat or Sometimes True   2 = Very True or Often True

0 1 2	57.	I physically attack people	0 1 2	84. I do things other people think are strange (describe):
0 1 2	58.	I pick my skin or other parts of my body (describe):		
0 1 2	59.	I can be pretty friendly	0 1 2	85. I have thought other people would think are strange (describe):
0 1 2	60.	I like to try new things		
0 1 2	61.	My school work is poor	0 1 2	86. I am stubborn
0 1 2	62.	I am poorly coordinated or clumsy	0 1 2	87. My moods or feelings change suddenly
0 1 2	63.	I would rather be with older kids than kids my own age	0 1 2	88. I enjoy being with people
0 1 2	64.	I would rather be with younger kids than kids my own age	0 1 2	89. I am suspicious
0 1 2	65.	I refuse to talk	0 1 2	90. I swear or use dirty language
0 1 2	66.	I repeat certain actions over and over; (describe):	0 1 2	91. I think about killing myself
			0 1 2	92. I like to make other laugh
			0 1 2	93. I talk too much
0 1 2	67.	I run away from home	0 1 2	94. I tease others a lot
0 1 2	68.	I scream a lot	0 1 2	95. I have a hot temper
0 1 2	69.	I am secretive or keep things to myself	0 1 2	96. I think about sex too much
0 1 2	70.	I see things that other people think aren't there (describe):	0 1 2	97. I threaten to hurt people
			0 1 2	98. I like to help others
			0 1 2	99. I smoke, chew or sniff tobacco
0 1 2	71.	I am self-conscious or easily embarrassed	0 1 2	100. I have trouble sleeping (describe):
0 1 2	72.	I set fires		
0 1 2	73.	I can work well with my hands	0 1 2	101. I cut classes or skip school
0 1 2	74.	I show off or clown	0 1 2	102. I don't have much energy
0 1 2	75.	I am too shy or timid	0 1 2	103. I am unhappy, sad or depressed
0 1 2	76.	I sleep less than most kids		
0 1 2	77.	I sleep more than most kids during day and/or night (describe):	0 1 2	104. I am louder than other kids
			0 1 2	105. I use drugs for nonmedical purposes (don't Include alcohol or tobacco) (describe):
0 1 2	78.	I am inattentive or easily distracted		
0 1 2	79.	I have a speech problem (describe):		
			0 1 2	106. I try to be fair to others
0 1 2	80.	I stand up for my rights	0 1 2	107. I enjoy a good joke
0 1 2	81.	I steal at home	0 1 2	108. I like to take life easy
0 1 2	82.	I steal from places other than home	0 1 2	109. I try to help others when I can
0 1 2	83.	I store up too many things I don't need (describe):	0 1 2	110. I wish I were of the opposite sex
			0 1 2	111. I keep from getting involved with others
			0 1 2	112. I worry a lot

Please write down anything else that describes your feelings, behaviour or interests

PLEASE BE SURE YOU ANSWERED ALL ITEMS

CORE System Initiative

The following information about the CORE system was modified for this publication by Chris Evans based on documentation by John Mellor-Clark. For more information, contact the CORE System Group at PTRC, University of Leeds, 17 Blenheim Terrace, Leeds LS2 9JT. Tel.: 0113 233 1990. Also see http://www.core-systems. co.uk for further information and sample copies of forms.

The CORE system was developed in a national collaborative research exercise to develop a standardised evaluation system for psychological therapies. The system involves two convenient tools and is based in the Psychological Therapies Research Centre [PTRC] in Leeds. It was launched nationally in 1998.

CORE Assessment & End of Episode Forms

This involves two forms, each on 2 sides of A4, completed by the therapists, which can be used for treatment evaluation and service audit. We believe this has several strengths.

- *Ease of completion* for **every** patient by **every** practitioner helps assure representative data.
- Forms provide routine *audit items* such as waiting times, appropriateness of referral and non-attendance rates as well as evaluative items.
- Forms initially included the *Health of the Nation Outcome Scales* [HoNOS] to address both the needs for service and patient profiling. Further developments have now created a more appropriate categorisation system based on over 2500 practitioner-provided descriptions of patient problems though the system is still compatible with HoNOS.
- Forms include *qualitative data* for referral reasons and ultimate post-therapy gains to complement to problem categorisation and fixed format responses.
- Forms collect proxies for *economic data* (e.g. medication, current and previous therapy) which is more reliably provided by practitioners than by patients.

- The forms include *therapy & service delivery descriptors* which can be related to outcomes.
- The data focus on issues which enhance patient assessment, therapy planning and patient discharge.

CORE Outcome Measure

This is a 34 item self-report questionnaire fitting on 2 sides of A4. It addresses the clinical domains of *subjective well-being* (4 items), *symptoms* (12 items including ones tapping anxiety, depression, trauma and physical symptoms), and *functioning* (12 items which include intimate relations, personal relations, social relations, and life functioning). In addition the measure contains 6 items which address components of *risk or harm* that can be clinical indicators of risk to self or to others. The measure is supported by two shorter (17 item) parallel versions to be used where a weekly or other high frequency of data collection is required. The measure has completed extensive trials and in primary, secondary and tertiary care psychotherapy and counselling settings has shown the following. (1) Clinical face value; (2) good internal and test-retest reliability; (3) concurrent validity against longer and expensive self-report measures and clinician ratings; and, (4) excellent effect size distinction between clinical and non-clinical samples. We believe the CORE Outcome Measure has the following advantages over measures in widespread current research use and some routine clinical use.

- As the measure is both *brief & user-friendly* (measured reading ease), patient compliance is high.
- The content of the measure addresses domains identified as routine assessment domains.
- The measure can be hand-scored easily or computer scanned.
- Existing *normative data* for clinical and non-clinical samples allow clinically significant and reliable change to be determined for each patient.
- As the measure is gaining national implementation a growing and substantial dataset of *comparative data* are becoming available.

- That dataset covers all levels of service delivery and hence allows collaborative comparison of similar services.

Practicalities of the CORE Evaluation System

- The CORE System uses *optical scanning* to mount data faster than manual entry hence summaries are available on a regular basis (e.g. every three months).
- As the CORE System is standardised, *automated reporting* is possible. This offers reports which will include individual practitioner feedback, practice feedback, service feedback, domain feedback and symptom group feedback.
- The CORE System links therapists to *a national practice research network* providing comparative data for a range of locations, disciplines and theoretical affiliations.

Further Reading & Supporting References

Barkham, M., Evans, C., Margison, F., McGrath, G., Mellor-Clark, J., Milne, D., & Connell, J. (1998). The rationale for developing and implementing core batteries in psychotherapy outcome research and clinical practice. *Journal of Mental Health*, 7(1): 35–47.

CORE System Group (1998) *CORE System (Information Management) Handbook*. Leeds: CORE System Group.

Mellor-Clark, J., & Barkham, M. (in press). Quality evaluation: methods, measures and meaning. In: C. Feltham & I. Horton (Eds), *The Handbook of Therapeutic Counselling*. London: Sage.

CORE Outcome Measures

CLINICAL

OUTCOMES in

ROUTINE

EVALUATION

OUTCOME MEASURE

Site ID — letters only | numbers only

Male ☐ Female ☐

Age

Client ID

Therapist ID | numbers only (1) | numbers only (2)

Sub codes

D D M M Y Y Y Y

Date form given

Stage Completed
S Screening
R Referral
A Assessment
F First Therapy Session
P Pre-therapy (unspecified)
D During Therapy
L Last therapy session
X Follow up 1
Y Follow up 2

Stage ☐

Episode ☐

IMPORTANT - PLEASE READ THIS FIRST

This form has 34 statements about how you have been OVER THE LAST WEEK.
Please read each statement and think how often you felt that way last week.
Then tick the box which is closest to this.
Please use a dark pen (not pencil) and tick clearly within the boxes.

Over the last week — (columns: Not at all | Only Occasionally | Sometimes | Often | Most or all the time | OFFICE USE ONLY)

1. I have felt terribly alone and isolated — ☐0 ☐1 ☐2 ☐3 ☐4 ☐F
2. I have felt tense, anxious or nervous — ☐0 ☐1 ☐2 ☐3 ☐4 ☐P
3. I have felt I have someone to turn to for support when needed — ☐4 ☐3 ☐2 ☐1 ☐0 ☐F
4. I have felt O.K. about myself — ☐4 ☐3 ☐2 ☐1 ☐0 ☐W
5. I have felt totally lacking in energy and enthusiasm — ☐0 ☐1 ☐2 ☐3 ☐4 ☐P
6. I have been physically violent to others — ☐0 ☐1 ☐2 ☐3 ☐4 ☐R
7. I have felt able to cope when things go wrong — ☐4 ☐3 ☐2 ☐1 ☐0 ☐F
8. I have been troubled by aches, pains or other physical problems — ☐0 ☐1 ☐2 ☐3 ☐4 ☐P
9. I have thought of hurting myself — ☐0 ☐1 ☐2 ☐3 ☐4 ☐R
10. Talking to people has felt too much for me — ☐0 ☐1 ☐2 ☐3 ☐4 ☐S
11. Tension and anxiety have prevented me doing important things — ☐0 ☐1 ☐2 ☐3 ☐4 ☐P
12. I have been happy with the things I have done. — ☐4 ☐3 ☐2 ☐1 ☐0 ☐F
13. I have been disturbed by unwanted thoughts and feelings — ☐0 ☐1 ☐2 ☐3 ☐4 ☐P
14. I have felt like crying — ☐0 ☐1 ☐2 ☐3 ☐4 ☐W

Please turn over

Over the last week

		Not at all	Only Occasionally	Sometimes	Often	Most or all the time	OFFICE USE ONLY
15	I have felt panic or terror	0	1	2	3	4	P
16	I made plans to end my life	0	1	2	3	4	R
17	I have felt overwhelmed by my problems	0	1	2	3	4	P
18	I have had difficulty getting to sleep or staying asleep	0	1	2	3	4	P
19	I have felt warmth or affection for someone	4	3	2	1	0	F
20	My problems have been impossible to put to one side	0	1	2	3	4	P
21	I have been able to do most things I needed to	4	3	2	1	0	F
22	I have threatened or intimidated another person	0	1	2	3	4	R
23	I have felt despairing or hopeless	0	1	2	3	4	P
24	I have thought it would be better if I were dead	0	1	2	3	4	R
25	I have felt criticised by other people	0	1	2	3	4	F
26	I have thought I have no friends	0	1	2	3	4	F
27	I have felt unhappy	0	1	2	3	4	P
28	Unwanted images or memories have been distressing me	0	1	2	3	4	P
29	I have been irritable when with other people	0	1	2	3	4	F
30	I have thought I am to blame for my problems and difficulties	0	1	2	3	4	P
31	I have felt optimistic about my future	4	3	2	1	0	W
32	I have achieved the things I wanted to	4	3	2	1	0	F
33	I have felt humiliated or shamed by other people	0	1	2	3	4	F
34	I have hurt myself physically or taken dangerous risks with my health	0	1	2	3	4	R

THANK YOU FOR YOUR TIME IN COMPLETING THIS QUESTIONNAIRE

Total Scores

Mean Scores
(Total score for each dimension divided by number of items completed in that dimension)

(W)	(P)	(F)	(R)	All items	All minus R

Tavistock and Portman NHS Trust Casenote Standards Criteria

1. Patient Details (PAS Front Sheet)
Responsibility: Department administrative staff

Front Sheet printed and attached to the inside of the file.	
Updated every time the status (on PAS) changes or when an audit is being carried out.	
All sections should be completed unless information is withheld or not applicable to the Department or particular case.	

2. Inserts
Responsibility: Department administrative staff

The full patient name should be on the first page of every insert	
The patient file number should be on the first page of every insert	

3. Clinical Information
Responsibility: Case Consultant

Frequency

A summary of the assessment interviews should be written within two weeks of completion	
A treatment update should be written at the end of every term	
A closing summary should be written within 28 days of the case being closed	

Format of all notes and letters in the file

All notes should be typed or written legibly	
Each entry should be fully dated	
All letters, reports and summaries should be signed and the author's name printed below	
The profession of the author should be stated except on letters to clients/families if not appropriate	

Content of Assessment Report

Reason for referral	
Service requested by referrer (if specified)	
Presenting problems	
Duration of problem	
Relevant family history	
Relevant medical and psychiatric/psychotherapeutic history	
Relevant school/work/career history	
Formulation (treatment specific e.g. psychodynamic)	
Recommendations (type of treatment/refer elsewhere etc.)	
Type of treatment offered including frequency	

Content of treatment updates

Current issues/concerns	
Progress of treatment and attendance	

Content of closing summary

Reason for closure	
Any ongoing/potential concerns	
Recommendations (for future care)	
Outcome	

Tavistock and Portman NHS Trust Referrer Communication Criteria

1. Initial contact
Responsibility: Intake

Ask for relevant information upon receipt of referral if sufficient information is not already given in the referral documents.	
Once referral received, inform the referrer.	

2. Format/content of Letters
Responsibility: Case Clinician

End of assessment letter (within two weeks of completion of assessment or three months after receipt of referral)	
Write in letter form (i.e. not bullet points)	
All letters to include patient name, current address and date of birth.	
Give date of first session.	
Give date of original referral.	
State number of times the patient has been seen to date.	
Give an outline of the main presenting problems.	
Give a formulation of the patient's difficulties.	
State the likely length and frequency of treatment.	

Follow up letters (to be sent at end of every term)	
Write in letter form.	
All letters to include patient name, current address and date of birth.	
Give date of previous letter.	
State regularity of attendance to date	
State progress of treatment (e.g. to continue/end date)	

Closure letter (to be sent to referrer within 4 weeks of case closure)	
Write in letter form.	
Letter to include patient name, current address and date of birth.	
Give date of original referral.	
State length of time seen and frequency.	
State patient's condition on termination (clinical outcome or current formulation).	
Give some indication of the patient's use of treatment.	
State availability of re-referral.	

3. Copying letters
Responsibility: Department Administrative Staff

If GP is not the referrer, all the above letters copied to the GP (if permission given)	

Confidentiality in Clinical Audit

Confidentiality of both patients and staff is a crucial aspect of the clinical audit process. The Data Protection Act of 1998 and the Caldicott Principles outline "the rules" regarding anyone processing personal data:

1. This data must be fairly and lawfully processed.
2. Processed for limited purposes
3. Adequate, relevant and not excessive
4. Accurate
5. Not kept longer than necessary
6. Processed in accordance with the patient's rights
7. Secure
8. Not transferred to places without adequate protection

The following are general guidelines surrounding the anonymity of patients, clinicians, and the Trust which should be adhered to at all times.

Patient Confidentiality
Individual patients have the right to confidentiality of their clinical records. In the clinical audit process, access to information identifying individual patients should be appropriately controlled and restricted by all staff involved in the project.

Staff Confidentiality
Members of staff have the right to expect that they will remain anonymous in a clinical audit project. If staff are happy about their names being published, you have to ensure that you have their full agreement: ensure that everyone has seen the final draft of the report.

Trust Confidentiality
The trust has the right to restrict results of clinical audit projects to authorised personnel only. However, in the vast majority of instances it is good practice to disseminate results widely, including external agencies and individuals.

Computer Confidentiality
The Data Protection Act (1984) prescribes that all information systems containing personal details must be registered with the Data Protection Registrar. However, there are certain exemptions fro the Data Protection Act for "Statistical and Research Data", and clinical audit systems can and do claim exemption, so long as they meet three conditions:

1. the data they hold must not be used for any purpose other than clinical audit or research.
2. The results of the project must not be made available in a form which identified the individual patients or staff.
3. The "raw" data must not be disclosed to anyone outside the Trust.

Confidentiality in the Office
Access to the office where the information is stored—either on computer or paper—ought to be controlled, and the room secured when unattended. It should not be possible for passers-by to see information on screens or printouts. Unwanted printed material should be disposed of securely, by shredding or incineration.

Disclosure of Clinical Audit Information to Patients
The Trust has the discretion either to or not to disclose audit information to patients. In some particular cases however, the Trust will seek legal ways to avoid disclosing sensitive information.

Treatment Choice in Psychological Therapies and Counselling

Principal Recommendations

- Psychological therapy should be routinely considered as an option when assessing mental health problems.

- Patients who are adjusting to life events, illnesses, disabilities or losses may benefit from brief therapies such as counselling.

- Post traumatic stress symptoms may be helped by psychological therapy, with most evidence for cognitive behavioural methods. Routine debriefing following traumatic events is not recommended.

- Depression may be treated effectively with cognitive therapy or interpersonal therapy. A number of other brief structured therapies for depression may be of benefit such as psychodynamic therapy.

- Anxiety disorders with marked symptomatic anxiety (panic disorder, agoraphobia, social phobia, obsessive compulsive disorders, generalised anxiety disorders) are likely to benefit from cognitive behaviour therapy.

- Psychological intervention should be considered for somatic complaints with a psychological component with most evidence for CBT in the treatment of chronic pain and chronic fatigue.

- Eating disorders can be treated with psychological therapy. Best evidence in bulimia nervosa is for CBT, IPT and family therapy for teenagers. Treatment usually includes psycho-educational methods. There is little strong evidence on the best therapy type for anorexia.

- Structured psychological therapies delivered by skilled practitioners can contribute to longer-term treatment of personality disorders.

The full document is available on the internet at www.doh.gov.uk/mentalhealth/treatmentguideline/leaflet.pdf

Mental Health Minimum Data Set

The table below lists all the items which make up the minimum data set. The table also identifies who is expected to provide the data at each stage of the Mental Health Care Spell. Note that each record relates to the activity occurring in the recording period to which it relates.

The table has been taken from:
Mental Health Minimum Data Set Data Manual Version 2.0, NHS Information Authority, July 2001

The MHMDS Implementation Team can be contacted on 020 7972 4996
Email: mb-mhmds@doh.gsi.gov.uk
NHSnet: nww.nhsia.nhs.uk/mentalhealth
Web: www.nhsia.nhs.uk/mentalhealth

DATA ITEM NAME	SOURCE
Reporting Period	
PATIENT DETAILS	
NHS Number	Entered at initial patient registration
Patient Electoral Ward	Derived from patient's postcode
Organisation Code (Health Authority)	Derived from Code of GP Practice and checked periodically
Sex	Entered at initial patient registration
Marital Status	Entered at initial patient registration; updated periodically by medical records staff
Birth Date	Entered at initial patient registration
Code Of GP Practice (Registered GMP)	Entered at initial patient registration
Organisation Code (Primary Care Group)	Derived from Code of GP Practice
Local Patient Identifier	Entered at initial patient registration
Social Services Identifier	Entered at initial patient registration
Ethnic Group	Entered at initial patient registration
Year Of First Mental Health Treatment	Entered at initial patient registration
MENTAL HEALTH CARE SPELL DETAILS	
Mental Health Care Spell Identifier	Entered automatically
Spell Number within Reporting Period	Entered automatically
Mental Health Specialty Function Code	Recorded for consultants. Entered automatically for patient based on consultant

Start Date	Entered by medical records staff
Source Of Referral: Mental Health	Entered by medical records staff
End Date	Entered usually by medical records staff
Mental Health Care Spell End Code	Entered usually by medical records staff or by health care practitioners as part of discharge process
Spell Days Within Reporting Period	Calculated from recording period and spell start and end date
Suspended Days Within Reporting Period	Calculated from recording period and start and end date of the suspension
Suspension Reason Code	Recorded when the Mental Health Care Spell is suspended, and indicates the type of provider treating the patient during the suspension
Days Of Standard CPA	Assumes CPA level defined explicitly at each CPA review and recorded probably by health care practitioner or medical secretary
Days Of Enhanced CPA	Assumes CPA level defined explicitly at each CPA review and recorded probably by health care practitioner or medical secretary
CPA Level At End Of Reporting Period	Assumes CPA level defined explicitly at each CPA review and recorded probably by health care practitioner or medical secretary
CPA Care Co-ordinator Occupation Code	Assumes patient's Care Co-ordinator recorded explicitly at CPA review
Date Last Saw Care Co-ordinator	Assumes identity of Care Co-ordinator recorded explicitly at CPA review and that contacts between Care Co-ordinator and patient recorded as part of on-going record of clinical contacts probably recorded by health care practitioner
Days Liable For Detention	Assumes that Mental Health Act administrator records change of status as they occur
Days Subject To Supervised Discharge	Assumes that Mental Health Act administrator records change of status as they occur
Legal Status At End Of Reporting Period	Assumes that Mental Health Act administrator records change of status as they occur
Most Restrictive Legal Status	Assumes that Mental Health Act administrator records change of status as they occur. Calculated from history of all legal statuses in reporting period
Care Without Patient Consent	Assumes that Mental Health Act administrator records change of status as they occur
Number Of Detention Assessments	Optional field. Included if contributed directly by Social Services department
Number Of Community Care Assessments	Optional field. Included if contributed directly by Social Services department

CARE PROGRAMME APPROACH ASSESSMENT DETAILS	
First Diagnosis (ICD10) NOTE: First to sixth diagnosis refers to electronic file order. Clinical encoding rules are not affected.	Assumes patient diagnosis recorded or confirmed explicitly at each CPA review, probably by health care practitioner or medical secretary. It should be possible to record or confirm up to 6 ICD10 diagnoses at each review
Second Diagnosis (ICD10) NOTE: First to sixth diagnosis refers to electronic file order. Clinical encoding rules are not affected.	Assumes patient diagnosis recorded or confirmed explicitly at each CPA review, probably by health care practitioner or medical secretary. It should be possible to record or confirm up to 6 ICD10 diagnoses at each review
Third Diagnosis (ICD10) NOTE: First to sixth diagnosis refers to electronic file order. Clinical encoding rules are not affected.	Assumes patient diagnosis recorded or confirmed explicitly at each CPA review, probably by health care practitioner or medical secretary. It should be possible to record or confirm up to 6 ICD10 diagnoses at each review
Fourth Diagnosis (ICD10) NOTE: First to sixth diagnosis refers to electronic file order. Clinical encoding rules are not affected.	Assumes patient diagnosis recorded or confirmed explicitly at each CPA review, probably by health care practitioner or medical secretary. It should be possible to record or confirm up to 6 ICD10 diagnoses at each review
Fifth Diagnosis (ICD10) NOTE: First to sixth diagnosis refers to electronic file order. Clinical encoding rules are not affected.	Assumes patient diagnosis recorded or confirmed explicitly at each CPA review, probably by health care practitioner or medical secretary. It should be possible to record or confirm up to 6 ICD10 diagnoses at each review
Sixth Diagnosis (ICD10) NOTE: First to sixth diagnosis refers to electronic file order. Clinical encoding rules are not affected.	Assumes patient diagnosis recorded or confirmed explicitly at each CPA review, probably by health care practitioner or medical secretary. It should be possible to record or confirm up to 6 ICD10 diagnoses at each review
First HoNOS In Mental Health Care Spell	Assumes HoNOS recorded explicitly at each CPA review, probably by health care practitioner or medical secretary
Date Of First HoNOS Rating	Assumes HoNOS recorded explicitly at each CPA review, probably by health care practitioner or medical secretary
Most Recent HoNOS	Assumes HoNOS recorded explicitly at each CPA review, probably by health care practitioner or medical secretary

Date Of Most Recent HoNOS Rating	Assumes HoNOS recorded explicitly at each CPA review, probably by health care practitioner or medical secretary
Best HoNOS In Reporting Period	Assumes HoNOS recorded explicitly at each CPA review, probably by health care practitioner or medical secretary. Choice of best in period undertaken automatically. Of relevance only to full year return
Date Of Best HoNOS Rating	Assumes HoNOS recorded explicitly at each CPA review, probably by health care practitioner or medical secretary
Worst HoNOS In Mental Health Care Spell	Assumes HoNOS recorded explicitly at each CPA review, probably by health care practitioner or medical secretary. Choice of worst in period undertaken automatically. Of relevance only to full year return
Date Of Worst HoNOS Rating	Assumes HoNOS recorded explicitly at each CPA review, probably by health care practitioner or medical secretary

MENTAL HEALTH CARE PACKAGE DETAILS

Psychiatric In-patient Bed Days	Calculated automatically from admission, discharge and period dates. Admission and discharge dates recorded probably by ward nursing or administrative staff
Medium Secure In-patient Bed Days	Calculated automatically from admission, discharge and period dates. Admission and discharge dates recorded probably by ward nursing or administrative staff during the ward or nursing home stays
Intensive Care In-patient Bed Days	Calculated automatically from admission, discharge and period dates. Admission and discharge dates recorded probably by ward nursing or administrative staff
Acute Home-Based Days	Calculated automatically from admission, discharge and period dates. Admission and discharge dates recorded probably by ward nursing or administrative staff
NHS Community Bed Days	Dates of admission and discharge from NHS residential care units entered either by nursing staff of community residential unit
Non-NHS Community Bed Use	Recorded at CPA review directly by clinical staff. Entered on system either by clinical staff or medical secretary
NHS Day Care Facility Attendances	Recorded at time of attendance by day care facility staff
Non-NHS Day Care Facility Use	Recorded at CPA review directly by clinical staff. Entered on system either by clinical staff or medical secretary